Slaves and slavery

Slaves and slavery

The British colonial experience

James Walvin

Manchester University Press
Manchester and New York

Distributed exclusively in the USA and Canada by St. Martin's Press

Copyright © James Walvin 1992

Published by Manchester University Press
Oxford Road, Manchester M13 9PL, UK
and Room 400, 175 Fifth Avenue, New York, NY 10010, USA

Distributed exclusively in the USA and Canada
by St. Martin's Press, Inc., 175 Fifth Avenue, New York, NY 10010, USA

British Library Cataloguing-in-Publication Data
A catalogue record for this book is available from the British Library

Library of Congress Cataloging-in-Publication Data
Walvin, James.
    Slaves and slavery : the British colonial experience / James
Walvin.
    p.   cm.
Includes bibliographical references.
ISBN 0-7190-3750-6 (cloth). – ISBN 0-7190-3751-4 (paper)
1. Slavery – Great Britain – Colonies – History. 2. Slave-trade-
Great Britain – History. I. Title.
HT1165.W35   1992
306.3'62'09171241 – dc20   92-8974

ISBN 0 7190 3750 6 *hardback*
      0 7190 3751 4 *paperback*

Printed in Great Britain
by Bell & Bain Limited, Glasgow

Contents

Preface

This is a small book which deals with a large topic. Over the past generation there has been a remarkable outpouring of scholarly research on black slavery in Africa and the Americas. The more detail we have, the clearer it has become that slavery was a central institution in the development of the Atlantic world in the seventeenth, eighteenth and nineteenth centuries. So vast a topic, which has spawned a voluminous and expanding literature, does not readily lend itself to a concise presentation.

In a book such as this, there will, inevitably, be omissions. More importantly perhaps, the simplicity of presentation does an injustice to the complex and sophisticated arguments of historians in the field. But I trust these shortcomings are more than offset by the virtues of bringing an important topic within range of a broader readership.

I must thank especially Avner Offer who read the first draft and subjected it to his distinctive scrutiny; it is a much better book for his efforts.

James Walvin
December 1991

1

Slavery in its context

This book attempts to describe, in broad outline, the history
of slavery and the slave trade in the British colonies up to
1838. In that year all slaves in British possessions were
freed. Those slaves were black, imported from Africa or
born to Africans and their descendants in the Americas.
Thus, the book concentrates on black slavery. It does not
seek to tell the story of slavery in the USA, although it is
concerned with slavery in the Northern American colonies
before they broke away from British control in 1776. This
book does not try to explain the course of slavery in the
non-English-speaking world, save only where it impinges
on the course of British slavery. It is, then, a brief account
of the British involvement with black slavery from the
early days of European colonisation through to the early
nineteenth century. Some attempt is then made to trace
the legacy of black slavery, a legacy which survives in a
host of ways today.

Many modern readers will simply assume that to speak
of slavery is to speak of black slavery. Yet it was only really
in the Americas that being black came to be associated
with slavery. In a myriad of societies, for centuries before
the first Africans were deposited in the Americas, slavery
had been commonplace. But it was not black slavery. The
modern western mind, however, automatically associates
slavery with the Africans imported into the Americas. In
part this is because the survivals of slavery are so obvious

[1]

in the western world. They are at their most obvious in the millions of descendants of slaves living in the USA and via West Indian immigration in Britain itself. There is also the historical legacy of black slavery in both Britain and the USA. And to add to the popular image, television (*Roots*) and a host of films have left indelible memories (some of them mythical) of black slavery and its role in recent western history firmly planted in the public mind.

There have been, to repeat, many other societies built on, or unquestioningly linked to slavery. At times it is easy to see who were the slaves and who were the slave-owners, but it was not always possible to distinguish the slave by race, colour, language or religion. Slaves often looked exactly like their owners. To add to the confusion facing historians, it is not always easy to define slavery. The line between freedom and slavery is sometimes blurred. It is also misleading to lump together all unfree peoples as slaves. There are some striking differences between unfree people. What, for example, distinguishes the lot of the black slave in eighteenth-century Virginia or Jamaica from the medieval serf, or indeed from the nineteenth-century Russian serf? It is now abundantly clear that there were great differences between black slave societies in the Americas; each colony had its own distinctive form of slavery and each form changed over time. Yet we are obliged to use the same words – slave and slavery – for a host of very different phenomena.

The form of slavery which Europeans created for their economic purposes in the Americas was different from other forms of slavery which had existed in the past. There was, of course, an awareness that slavery had existed before. The Spaniards and Portuguese had legal traditions, derived from Roman law, which made special provision for slaves. And most early modern European societies had been built on forms of feudalism in which large numbers of people were unfree.

Slavery was basic to the world of classical antiquity from approximately 1000 BC to AD 500. Greek and Roman law and economic usage confirm the importance of slavery in a number of important ways. Slaves were used not merely as beasts of burden (in the mines for instance), but were to be counted among the great craftsmen of Athens and Rome. As those two empires expanded, slaves were imported from the peripheries to the imperial heartlands; there were thriving slave trades long before that which spanned the Atlantic. By the time of Christ there were perhaps 2–3 million slaves in the area of modern Italy: perhaps 35–40 per cent of the population. Roman slaves were the foundation of local agriculture and were sold along with the land, the animals and the buildings. This was to happen throughout the Americas. There were contemporary criticisms of classical slavery, though they generally went unheeded. Slavery was a highly successful system (or systems) which lasted for centuries and clearly brought material well-being to both Greece and Rome. It is worth noting that black slavery in the Americas lasted for only half the time that classical slavery endured (M.L. Finley, 1968; T. Wiedemann, 1981).

There were other forms of slavery in Europe following the disintegration of the Roman Empire. The Vikings, the Anglo-Saxons and the Normans controlled large servile populations. Indeed, it seems likely that the great majority of the people of medieval Europe were unfree, sharing the hereditary status of serfs. Tied to the land, owning few material possessions, inherited and bequeathed like other forms of goods, serfs were tied to the land for generations. Yet they were not slaves, and few contemporaries thought of them as such. Moreover European feudalism had a great

[3]

variety of local forms (P. Bonnassie, 1991). But at its heart lay its dependence upon an unfree population. The serfs, said the Bishop of Laon in 1025, form 'a miserable race which owns nothing that it does not get by its own labour. Who can calculate the toil by which the serfs are absorbed? Their long journeys, their labours? Money, clothing and food – all are provided by the serfs. Not one man could live without them.' (R. Hilton, 1973, 54.)

The rise of serfdom witnessed a parallel decline of European slavery (though domestic slavery lingered on, notably in a number of Italian cities). Yet before the Europeans had begun those maritime voyages which drew them towards Africa and ultimately to African slavery, European feudalism was in decline. This was especially true in England. In the years when Europeans made their first tentative steps towards colonisation of the New World, the Old World was in the process of shedding its broadly-based attachment to unfree labour. It was to be one of many striking ironies in the subsequent history of black slavery that nations which prided themselves on their freedoms were, at precisely the same time, taking their first steps towards developing a more complete form of slavery for growing numbers of other peoples. But those new slaves were black and they were to be shipped from their African homelands into the Americas.

2

European expansion and the origins of black slavery

Black slavery existed long before the development of the Atlantic slave trade: long before Europeans began to make profitable commerce in shipping Africans from their home-lands to the Americas. Yet we need to ask: why and how did Europeans first begin to involve themselves in the affairs of a continent so removed from their immediate interests and, apparently so distant from their commercial trade routes?

Europeans had known about Africa for centuries, but much of their knowledge had been inherited through a mixed tradition of rumour, myths and elements of classical learning. There was, for instance, a host of biblical refer-ences and allusions to the mysteries of black Africa. More tangible was the legacy of ancient trade and empires which bound together the worlds of Africa and Europe. The trading world of the Phoenicians, for instance, linked the towns and societies of the eastern Mediterranean and North Africa with a number of southern European cities (M. Bernal, 1987). Later the culture of classical Greece expanded the ties between mainland Europe and parts of Africa. But by 150 BC the emergent power of Rome had conquered Greece and a new empire – the Roman Empire – began to exert its power throughout the Mediterranean and Europe. North Africa was incorporated into that Empire. The wealth of the Nile valley was tapped for imperial benefit, Roman towns were developed across North Africa, and this enormous region came to play an important economic role within the broad framework of the Roman Empire. It was an empire which stretched from the settlements of northern Europe to the black peoples of the Nile and the southern Sahara.

One important link between Europe and Africa was Christianity. We need to remember that Christianity emerged from and developed during the Roman Empire. It was a cult of the eastern Empire, centred initially on Antioch, Constantinople and Alexandria as well as Rome. But it also moved south, through Syria, Egypt, south to Nubia and Ethiopia. While we are familiar with the Christianisation of northern Europe, it is important to recall that this region shared a faith with other peoples – non-white peoples – who lived on the fringes of the world known to northern Europeans. Christians in northern Europe belonged to a fraternity which incorporated, at its most southerly fringe, black Africans.

Religion was not the sole ancient link between Europe and black Africa. Trade was perhaps the most important tie. Trade across the Mediterranean brought many of the goods and commodities from sub-Saharan Africa into the market places and (more prosperous) homes of Western Europe. Gold, frankincense (used in Roman funeral pyres) and myrhh (used in cosmetics) were African goods, the latter two from the Horn of Africa and southern Arabia (P. D. Curtin, 1978, 63: 1990). These and a host of products from Roman North Africa and even further afield were fed into mainland Europe.

Links between Europe and Africa were then ancient and well-tested. And these ties across the Mediterranean had been forged to a marked degree by the various empires – Phoenician, Greek and Roman – which had conquered or controlled parts of the Meditteranean.

From the mid-seventh century AD a new empire began

[6]

to exert its own distinctive power over the Mediterranean. Within a century Islam reached from the borders of India and China, through Arabia to embrace the eastern Mediterranean, North Africa and Spain. Western Europe seemed, by the mid-eighth century AD, to be pinned back by an aggressive and successful empire. The Islamic grip on North Africa henceforth effectively cut Europe off from those trans-Saharan trading routes to the peoples and goods of black Africa.

Islam began to spread into black Africa. Carried via merchants and traders, Islam began to take root in West Africa, the Horn of Africa and the Sudan. Like Phoenicians and Greeks before them, Islamic traders were the transmitters of religion as well as of goods and chattels. Centuries later, European adventurers were to play a similar role for Christianity. By 1500 a vast Islamic trading system had established itself throughout West Africa, fanning out from Timbuktu in the north to Gambia in the west and down to Benin in the south-west. Through these complex routes, the goods – and sometimes the peoples – of black Africa were brought in contact with the cultures of the Mediterranean. Like empires before and since, this Islamic trading empire involved a marked migration of people; people moved by choice, for a host of economic and social reasons, and people moved because they were slaves and had no choice in the matter.

Slaves were common in the Islamic regions of black Africa. Often the victims of warfare and subsequently sold and force-marched far from their native regions, slaves were to be found littering the heartland of Islamic West Africa. And they were, of course, the basis for an export trade in slaves from black Africa across the Sahara to North Africa (P.D. Curtin, 1978, 95–6; Lovejoy, 1983, Ch.2). But slavery was not unique to Islamic Africa. Forms of slavery abounded throughout black Africa, but they were forms of slavery which were utterly different from the slavery which came into being with the development of the Americas. Indeed, many students of Africa have argued that the very concept of slavery – suffused as it is in the West with images of and associations with black chattel slavery in the Americas – is simply an inappropriate word or concept for the forms of bondage to be found in black Africa before the white incursions. This complex topic – one of continuing and fierce debate – need not distract us (S. Miers and I. Kopytoff, 1983, Intro.; P. Lovejoy, 1983, Ch. 1; P. Manning, 1990).

When Europeans made their first tentative steps as explorers or merchant-adventurers in West Africa, they discovered relationships between Africans which looked like – and which they described as – slavery. They simply assumed that African slavery was established before they arrived. It is important to recall, however, that Europeans subsequently transformed black slavery out of all previous recognition.

Other forms of bondage had been common in various black African societies even before the impact of Islam. Often, local forms of slavery were marginal to the way society functioned. Historians have identified a number of forms of 'dependency' which fall short of any useful definition of slavery in pre-modern Africa; pawnship (holding a person for debts), certain forms of marriage and concubinage, and specific roles in local religions (for sacrifice, for instance) (P. Lovejoy, 1983, 11–15; Patterson, 1982). What Islam did was to disperse black African slaves throughout a much broader geographical setting. Black slaves were fed into a range of positions and jobs throughout Islamic society.

Slaves were taken as prisoners of war; women and

[8]

children were more popular than men, and were used for domestic work or for sexual purposes. In time, slaves came to occupy a range of occupations throughout the Islamic world of the Mediterranean, working as soldiers, officials, eunuchs and more generally in administration. Slaves were recruited and maintained as 'pagans' (they were not converted) and hence a regular and continuing need for fresh supplies of new slaves was soon created.

Islamic merchants gathered black Africans together and moved them north, across the Sahara, up the East African coast or along the Red Sea. This trade in slaves remained quite small, no more perhaps than a few thousand per year. Compared to what was to follow, this was the slightest of human trickles north from black Africa. And because it was so small and spread over so vast a region, the Islamic slave trade is not thought to have created major transformations in the societies of black Africa. All this was to change with the arrival of the Europeans.

It is worth repeating the point. Slavery, however defined, had existed in black Africa before Europeans arrived. Moreover, black Africans had long been familiar – if exotic – sights in Europe (especially in Mediterranean societies) before Europeans began their maritime voyages to West Africa. It is equally true that the European presence was to transform black slavery into a unique institution in the development of the broader Atlantic economy. But why should the Europeans find themselves attracted to black Africa in the first place?

European society had long been familiar with images – real or mythological – of black Africa. There had been, for instance, a flourishing iconography of black people throughout European painting and sculpture. Images of black Africans had adorned countless European pictures and icons for centuries. The Negro was a commonplace sight in European art from the world of classical antiquity through to the early Renaissance (F. Snowden, 1983).

Nor was this black presence simply a matter of pictures or images. Africans had long been resident in Europe, especially in those Mediterranean societies with direct links to North Africa (and thence to black Africa). Africans were common sights in Moslem Spain in the eleventh and twelfth centuries and there, as elsewhere, were to be found in the epic literature and iconography of chivalry. Similarly Africans found their way, often via Sicily, into the major cities and states of the Italian mainland.

It was scarcely surprising, given the size of the Roman Empire, that people from one imperial periphery would find their way to another. Africans were often used in the armies of the Empire and were, inevitably, stationed throughout the widely-scattered imperial outposts. There were, for instance, African soldiers in the Roman armies which occupied the south of Britain for more than three centuries. There was even a division of 'Moors' on Hadrian's Wall in the third century AD (P. Fryer, 1984, 1–2).

In the Middle Ages there were other small movements of Africans north to Europe, some being sold as slaves through Genoa, Naples or Barcelona. Africans only began to arrive in Europe in significant numbers in the fifteenth century, and only then because of the growing importance and frequency of maritime links between Europe and West Africa. For the first time the old fragmentary links overland and thence across the Mediterranean were by-passed and a direct route opened from black Africa to Europe. To understand why that happened we need to switch our focus to Europe itself.

European maritime expansion was in large part a result of the major changes in European society and economy. There had for centuries been long and tortuous overland

trade routes linking Europe to the wider world. But in the
fifteenth century Europeans, led by the Portuguese, broke
the traditional bonds which had effectively tied them to
trade and travel in Europe and the Mediterranean. In what
historians have called the 'Age of Reconnaissance', a combination of forces encouraged Europeans to sail beyond the
bounds of their known world. There was first of all the
commercial and financial imperative: the need for exotic
goods and trade, and the knowledge that they were available, but only well beyond the confines of traditional
mercantile ventures.

The search for precious metals and spices prompted the
remarkably swift opening of the outside world to European
penetration. Gold and spices had long arrived in Europe via
the overland routes to Africa and Asia, but the extraordinary
problems of such routes – and their frequent insecurity and
unreliability – prompted the urge to look for sea routes.

Money from traditional capitalists in the old Mediterranean commercial centres financed exploratory voyages,
mainly by Spaniards and Portuguese (J. H. Parry, 1963, Ch.
2; P. D. Curtin, 1990, Ch. 2). Long distance sailing became
more commonplace as the fifteenth century advanced. We
can list the various improvements in ship design, in naviga-
tional instruments and astronomical tables and charts
which ultimately transformed ocean sailing, although
many of the early voyages of discovery used older, simpler
techniques: the compass, the experience of sailing, and
dead-reckoning (J. H. Hale, 1971, 48–9). But there was
undoubtedly a growing curiosity about the nature of the
world's geography – about how it might reflect what was
known from an ancient cartographical tradition. There
was a dawning realisation that vast tracts of the world –
notably Africa – might be circumnavigable.

There was, then, an element of intellectual curiosity

involved, though it was a curiosity born of commercial, and to a degree religious zeal: the need to seek maritime access to valuable trade routes and the related urge to outflank the resistant barriers of the Islamic world. The Portuguese were the pioneers, their sailors – often of other nationalities – edging their way down and along the African coast. They moved 'cape by cape and beach by beach, from the security of the known' (J.H. Hale, 1971, 51). When they rounded the Cape and encountered Mozambique there was laid out before them the commercial and trading experience of the Indian Ocean. The way was open to India and the Far East. Before then, other Europeans were coming to terms with their discoveries on the coast of West Africa.

We know of the more famous voyages to Africa, but many others went unrecorded in the search for fishing and trade. Gossip among European sailors quickly established the region as an attractive – if dangerous and speculative – region for trade, its gold, spices and peoples valuable or merely objects of curiosity.

By 1460 the Portuguese had settled in Madeira and the Azores and had penetrated south to Sierra Leone. A decade later they were further south on the Guinea Coast and the Bight of Benin. They established stations at crucial points, at El Mina (Gold Coast, 1481) and Axim (Ivory Coast, 1503), the very names an indicator that commodities other than slaves were the prime attraction.

By the end of the century the Portuguese had claimed the island of São Tomé in the Gulf of Guinea. There they built plantations to grow sugar cane for Europe. They used Africans as slaves, imported from neighbouring regions (Gabon, for instance, was only 200 miles away). But why slaves?

Although we are often tempted to associate sugar cane

[12]

with the plantations of the West Indies, cane cultivation had moved westwards from its native homeland in the east. One result of the march of Islam was the creation of sugar production throughout their settlements in the Mediterranean. Cane cultivation shifted slowly westwards, from India, through Persia and then into settlements in North Africa and southern Europe. Sugar was grown in Crete, Cyprus, Malta, Rhodes, Sicily, Morocco and Spain, and was traded through the major international marketing cities, notably Venice. Thus it is important to stress that the European taste for cane sugar was well established long before the opening of the plantations in the Americas. It is also worth noting that in many of those early sugar-growing regions, the labour was undertaken by slaves.

By the time the Portuguese began to experiment with sugar production in their homeland, much of the Mediterranean sugar industry was in decline (S. Mintz, 1985, Ch. 2). What was to transform this crop – and ultimately to transform the history of the whole Atlantic region – was the creation of sugar plantations in the newly-acquired Atlantic islands.

The Spaniards and the Portuguese began to cultivate cane in their Atlantic islands of Madeira, the Canaries and São Tomé. Initially, their output – and the quality of their sugar – accelerated the decline of the sugar industry in the Mediterranean. Yet these were the very years when European taste and demand for sugar was growing. European settlers on those islands, backed by outside financiers and entrepreneurs, established modern plantations. For labour, they turned to the readily available supplies of Africans on the nearby African coast. By enterprising marketing, this new product greatly enhanced European demand for sugar. The Atlantic islands were, however, more than merely experimental market gardens:

they gave the Portuguese a vital base for the continuing exploration of the African coastline; they made possible the rounding of Africa, and they provided effective control of the South Atlantic (S. Mintz, 1985, 30–31).

The plantations in the Atlantic islands used slaves as labourers. It was formerly thought that this labour tradition was simply transferred from the industries in the Mediterranean, but it now seems that many of the new plantations used a mixture of free and slave labour. Slaves were undoubtedly important, but so too were the free labourers – some specialists and some wage labourers. This mix of labour – free and enslaved – was to be common in the early days of settlement throughout the Americas, from Barbados to Virginia. It is clear that there was, initially at least, nothing 'natural' about the African which rendered him/her ideal for work on this tropical or semi-tropical crop. Nor was work in sugar a task which only slaves could do; free white men worked alongside black slaves in the cane fields (S. Mintz, 1985, 32).

By 1500 the Portuguese had effectively opened up a coastline of some 4,000 miles, had established a string of forts to be used as entrepôts, and had secured bases in the Atlantic islands, especially in São Tomé and Príncipe in the Gulf of Guinea, from which to trade to and from the African coast. The Portuguese sought to exclude outside interests from this massive and potentially invaluable region. Although the Portuguese initially prized the region's gold, this urge to exclude competitors (on the part of all involved) was to be a feature of Atlantic trade for centuries. And this was to be the case, even when it became clear that African slaves were even more valuable than gold itself. A Treaty of 1494 divided the Atlantic world between Spain and Portugal; Portugal was awarded Africa, Asia and Brazil, Spain the rest of the New World.

Thus was Spain excluded from Africa and the subsequently lucrative slave trade.

The Portuguese turned to Africa for much of their labouring requirements on their island settlements. By 1500 perhaps a thousand had been landed in São Tomé, another 7,500 into the Atlantic islands – but an astonishing 25,000 in mainland Europe (J. Rawley, 1981, 24; H. Klein, 1986). Imported mainly into Portugal, Africans, employed in a range of services – but mainly used as exotic, eye-catching domestics – were soon to be found throughout Europe; they were more numerous and more noticeable than in any previous era. But it was São Tomé which saw the most dramatic changes wrought by African imports.

The Africans of São Tomé were the instruments for the economic revolution on the island. By 1600 some 76,000 had been imported, set to work on large and increasingly sophisticated estates, fed and clothed by European imports, the produce of their labours marketed through Antwerp, and their owners/employers able to lead a lavish lifestyle which was, in time, to be the hallmark of the New World planters.

The 'discovery' of the New World was of course part of the broader urge to explore the unknown world. Like some of the major West African explorations, it also sprang from a desire to seek a trading route to the Indies: to find a maritime link to the source of so much real and fabled wealth. Most famous of all, of course, were the voyages of Columbus, son of a poor Genoese weaver, with some experience of voyages to the Guinea coast and dispatched in 1492 to 'discover and acquire islands and mainland in the ocean sea'. As early as 1484 Columbus had suggested a western voyage to Asia to the Portuguese Crown. But it was under the flag of Castille that he finally crossed the Atlantic in 1492, and after thirty-three days made landfall in the Bahamas before threading his way south-west to Cuba and

Hispaniola (Haiti). On his second voyage, in 1493, Columbus and his Spanish backers were fortified by a recent Papal Bull which effectively granted Spain all lands to be discovered 'beyond the line' (a line drawn north to south 100 leagues west of the Azores and Cape Verde Islands). Subsequent negotiations between Spain and Portugal conceded the area to be known as Brazil to Portugal, and the rest of the New World to Spain. Columbus now touched land in the Lesser Antilles, passed Puerto Rico and Hispaniola and proceeded thence to Cuba and Jamaica. On his third voyage in 1498 he touched Trinidad and Venezuela before heading north to Hispaniola.

These explorations were the first of many, as Europeans sought routes to the East. But they discovered instead a vast new continent, 'a new world, so distant is it and so devoid of civilization and religion'. By the turn of the century this vast New World was being valued for its own sake: for its prospects and potential, and for the wealth it had already begun to yield – gold, pearls, dye-woods, fisheries, and land for settlement in abundance. 'What need have we of what is found everywhere in Europe?,' asked one explorer (J. H. Parry, 1963, 154–5).

It was, however, ironic that one of the earliest discoveries was not indigenous to the Americas. Europeans soon realised that sugar could easily be grown in a number of places in the Americas. On his second voyage, Columbus carried sugar cane from the Canaries to Hispaniola. By 1516 the first American sugars, from Santo Domingo, were shipped back to Europe. And this new sugar industry was worked by enslaved Africans.

Ten years later Brazil shipped sugar back to Lisbon. Soon sugar was being grown throughout the region: in Mexico, Paraguay, on the Pacific coast of South America – indeed, wherever conditions seemed favourable. As indigenous

[16]

labour declined – succumbing in the main to newly-imported European diseases – Africans were imported to undertake the labour. Often they were supervised by skilled men experienced in sugar manufacture in the Atlantic islands. Aided by the state, Spanish settlers set up plantations in Santo Domingo, Cuba, Puerto Rico and Jamaica. Yet it was a promising industry which swiftly came to an end; settlers moved on to other regions in search of precious metals, and the pioneering sugar industry collapsed (S. Mintz, 1985, 32–3).

Basic to the Spanish experience in that pioneering sugar industry were the black slaves imported across the Atlantic. Using Africans as slaves was, as we have seen, not new when the Europeans began to settle the Americas. They had been common in Portugal and were especially important in the Atlantic islands. As New World settlement proceeded, and as slaves became ever more important in the peopling and economic transformation of the region, the right to supply slaves from Africa became an increasingly valuable form of trade. The Portuguese had an effective monopoly in bases on the African coast. They alone had the organisation and ability, for much of the sixteenth century, to dispatch Africans in any significant numbers to their fate across the Atlantic. Only they had tested dealings with African slave traders away from the coast. And to capitalise on this monopoly the *asiento*, a license, granted permission to Portuguese slavers, to transport Africans (J. Rawley, 1981, 26).

This controlled system could never satisfy demand for fresh slaves. There was, for one thing, a shortage of shipping. More important, interlopers and rival states were forever eager to secure some part of the trade for themselves. The first English slave trading venture was Sir John Hawkins' famous voyage of 1562, when, with furtive royal backing, he sailed to Tenerife, then to Sierra Leone and 'got into his possession, partly by the sword, and partly by other means, to the number of 300. Negros at the least'. He sailed to Hispaniola, sold the slaves and other goods to the Spaniards: 'And so with prosperous successe and much gaine to himselfe and the afforesayde adventurers, he came home' (Hakluyt, 1926, VII, 5–6). Thereafter, English traders – and the English Court – found the lucrative prospects of the slave trade irresistible.

It was, however, the Portuguese Empire which had the greatest appetite for slaves. Brazil, claimed by the Portuguese in 1500, offered unimaginable room for settlement and expansion. At the point where Brazil is closest to Africa there were ideal conditions for sugar production. At first the Portuguese settlers, like the Spaniards before them, enslaved Indians to work in the sugar fields. And again like the Spaniards, this labour experiment failed. The Indians fled, rebelled or, more likely, died: victims of European disease more than European economic exploitation (S. Schwartz, 1986). Indians could not, or would not, work as the new Brazilian settlers wanted and demanded. It was perfectly understandable, therefore, that Brazilian sugar growers should turn to the form of labour already tried and tested in the Atlantic islands, in Portugal itself and, briefly, in the Spanish Americas.

Africans had been allowed in as imports in 1549; in the 1570s their numbers increased rapidly. By 1600 there were 13–15,000 blacks in Brazil, the majority of them labouring on the country's 130 sugar plantations. Thereafter, and for the best part of three centuries, Brazil was to consume Africans like no other region in the Americas. By 1870 an estimated 4,190,000 Africans had been deposited in Brazil (J. Rawley, 1981, 27–9, 428; J.C. Miller, 1988). Even as early as 1600, perhaps 50,000 slaves had been landed in

[18]

Brazil. By the same date more than a quarter of a million Africans had been taken from their various homelands and scattered to the far-flung regions of Europe and European settlements across the Atlantic. Yet as staggering as this figure may seem, it was but a foretaste of what was to come.

The expansion of Europe beyond the seas was, as we have seen, a function of the internal history of Europe itself. This early phase of expansion had been closely bound to the expansive strength of Spain and Portugal. Following the union of those two Crowns in 1580, Portugal was dragged into conflict with the Dutch, the rising northern European power. It was a conflict which was to transform the subsequent history of slavery and the slave trade.

Dutch financial strength, their maritime power and their aggressive commercial outlook severely dented the Portuguese dominance of Atlantic trade and settlement. In a war which lasted until 1648, the Dutch managed to occupy (sometimes briefly) the Portuguese possessions in West Africa, Angola, the West Indies and Brazil. Much of this loss was regained, but the Portuguese were now facing increasingly powerful rivals. Those rivals – notably the Dutch and the English – also wanted land in the New World and plentiful supplies of Africans to work it. And even more than that of the late sixteenth century, seventeenth-century expansion was fuelled by the rise of sugar.

Dutch financial backing and trading expertise proved crucial in the rapid growth of the Brazilian sugar industry. As slaves were poured into Brazil, their owners rose to dizzying heights of wealth and opulence, personifying – especially to Europeans – the gaudy and vulgar wealth it was possible to create in the Americas. Sugar rescued the Portuguese economy, made a number of Brazilian ports into major centres and, of course, led to a more ruthless and widespread scouring of the African coastline for black labour. Brazilian sugar amounted to 16,300 tons in 1600; by 1650 it was 28,500 tons. Slaves were being sought throughout Angola; Luanda now replaced São Tomé as the major African slave market.

Throughout the seventeenth century the most important Atlantic slaving link was between Angola and Brazil. Almost all the Africans taken across the Atlantic in that century were carried to Brazil, the bulk of them destined for the burgeoning sugar industry. But, as we shall see in other parts of the Americas, slaves were soon being used at all levels of the economy and were not used solely as beasts of burden.

It is important to stress the crucial role of the Portuguese in establishing and developing the trade in African slaves and in proving the value of slaves in the Americas. It seemed to outsiders that here was a lucrative trade; the benefits of slave-grown sugar seemed irrefutable and could be illustrated by the rise of material prosperity in Brazil, among the slave traders themselves and in the benefits accruing to Portugal. Set against this remarkable rise to prosperity, few voices could be heard pleading for the African slaves.

For all the undoubted wealth of the Portuguese empire in Brazil, it was Spain which laid claim to most of the Americas. Yet theirs was an empire which was difficult to defend and was concerned as much with precious metals as with producing tropical staples. By 1600 the Spanish possessions had consumed the largest volume of slaves, perhaps 75,000. By the end of slavery, Spanish America had absorbed some 1,700,000 Africans (something like one-sixth of all the Atlantic trade). The most important destination was Cuba, followed, a long way behind, by Mexico (J. Rawley, Ch. 11).

Initially the Spaniards had tried Indian labour, in the mines and in the fields. But it did not work, for much the same reason it did not work in Brazil. The drift to African

slave labour was hastened by the Church defending local
Indians and by the fact that traditional Spanish law recognised slavery. It was not so startling a change of fortunes for
the Spaniards to turn to slave labour. But it also seemed the
obvious and necessary thing to do, given the catastrophic
collapse of the indigenous local population. Africans, often
immune to many of the diseases which killed the Indians,
were ferried across the Atlantic in growing numbers, the
bulk of them from Upper Guinea and Angola, before the
mid-seventeenth century.

By that time, however, the Spanish Empire was under
severe threat from other European quarters, notably from
the Dutch, the English and the French. All those three
nations were strong where Spanish was growing weaker: all
had ambitions for trade and settlement beyond the seas; all
had traditions of merchant adventuring, and all had an
unsated lust for the prosperity and possessions of their
European rivals. The slave colonies, and the right to supply
them with Africans, were to be a source and cause of friction,
warfare and diplomatic wrangles from that day forward.
Indeed, the slave colonies were to become prized possessions over which Europeans feuded for centuries. The
Europeans projected on to the islands and the land mass of
North and South America each successive phase of tensions
and rivalries within Europe itself. And by the early seventeenth century the Spanish Empire proved too seductive for
emergent European powers to resist.

Spain was under regular attack or pressure throughout
the early seventeenth century, its Empire hopelessly
exposed to the settlements of rival Europeans. The French,
urged by an aggressive government keen to seek the obvious
benefits of New World settlement, settled Guadaloupe and
Martinique, the Dutch took Curaçao (to become a vital
entrepôt), and the English began a long process of settlement

and consolidation throughout the Caribbean. All three countries also established their own bases in West Africa. Thereafter the slave trade was to change fundamentally, and much of the trading across the Atlantic shifted to the 'new' European powers.

What gave these countries their strength to embark on conquest and settlement in the Americas was their political stability and commercial power. Holland had long been a formidable mercantile nation, with remarkable networks of trade, banking and insurance centred on Amsterdam. They soon became the financiers and shippers of the seventeenth-century slave trade. And their commercial expertise, when harnessed to their experience in the sugar industry in Brazil, was to be the basis for the transformation of the Caribbean into a major sugar producer.

The English had been keen to embark on sugar production from the early seventeenth century. It has been tried unsuccessfully in Bermuda in 1616 and in Virginia after 1619. Not able to grow it, the English plundered sugar (along with all other forms of booty) from the Spaniards. But the English, settlement of Barbados in 1625 proved the turning point. For the next twenty years the island – and other West Indian islands acquired in the period – was converted to sugar production. By the time the English seized Jamaica from the Spanish in 1655, sugar was a thriving concern in Barbados. And all the time the English taste for sugar grew apace. The English quickly learned the techniques of sugar production from the Dutch, and the plantation system leapt from island to island throughout the British Caribbean. As British sugar got cheaper, the old-established Portuguese dominance of the northern European sugar business was replaced by the British.

In 1660, the British imported 1,000 hogshead of sugar; by 1700 it had risen to 50,000 and thirty years later was

100,000. What had happened was the extraordinary expansion of domestic British consumption of sugar. Of course, these were also the years of a remarkable growth in domestic British consumption of all manner of material things (N. McKendrick, 1983; C. Shammas, 1990). It was in these years that the British developed their famous 'sweet tooth'. There were a number of important factors which went to create this remarkable transformation. But none of it could have happened without those armies of black slaves whose labours tapped the luxuriant tropical fields for the sweet substance of international trade and domestic taste.

On the eve of the English conquest of Jamaica, in the mid-seventeenth century, it was abundantly clear that slaves were the key to colonial prosperity in the tropics. Slaves were the human hinge on which the broader Altantic slaving system pivoted. 'To obtain them, products were shipped to Africa; by their labour power, wealth was created in the Americas. The wealth they created mostly returned to Britain; the products they made were consumed in Britain; and the products made by Britons – cloth, tools, torture-instruments – were consumed by slaves who were themselves consumed in the creation of wealth.' (S. Mintz, 1985, 43.) Barbados was described thus in 1645: 'you shall see a flourishing Island, many able men, I believe they have brought this year no less than a thousand Negroes, and the more they buy the better able they are to buy, for in a year and a half they will earn (with God's blessing) as much as they cost' (M. Craton, 1974, 43). It was this slave-based economy which was to transform the West Indies, enrich Britain and to drain vast reaches of Africa of much of its human strength.

3

British slavery

England's rise to the status of major slaving nation in the seventeenth century was rooted in her possession of a string of West Indian islands (and, to a lesser extent, her colonies in North America). But the ability to become a major imperial power was itself a reflection of commercial and maritime power. England was ideally placed to launch into overseas ventures. Its population was expanding, there was a thriving rural industry (based on cloth production and export) and there was a wage economy in both town and country. But poverty was also increasing (and had been since Elizabeth's time), so labour was mobile and moved across the face of the nation in search of work. When, in the early seventeenth century, the opportunity arose to cross the Atlantic, many Britons, especially the poor and the young, took the opportunity to migrate. English society was perhaps the most dynamic in Europe, and its willingness to migrate soon made possible the remarkable development of English colonies in the Caribbean and in North America (B. Bailyn and P.D. Morgan, eds., 1991).

In Barbados, the first ten years of English settlement concentrated on tobacco cultivation; it was a profitable business which attracted further migrations from Britain. But from the 1640s Barbadian planters began to turn to sugar. This crop was both capital and labour intensive; land-holdings grew larger and were more intensively worked. Free white labourers were gradually replaced by African slaves. By the 1650s the population density of Barbados was greater than any other English area except London. As sugar became king, the number of whites declined (from 30,000 in 1650 to 15,500 in 1700). And the island also became ever more African. The spread of sugar cultivation throughout the English islands – St Kitts, Nevis, Montserrat, Antigua and Barbados – was prompted in large part by Dutch money, experience and expertise. And local planters tended to buy their Africans from the Dutch slave traders. By the turn of the century, Barbados was home to more than 41,000 slaves (R. S. Dunn, 1972, 87). Barbados a mere half century after its settlement was 'the richest, most highly developed, most populous, and most congested English colony in America' (J. P. Greene, 1988, 44).

The sugar industry was dominated by perhaps 200 major planters who owned sizeable plantations. But their lands were now worked by Africans. The initial dependence upon indentured British labour (often from Scotland or Ireland) was in decline. Black and white had, in the early years of settlement, worked side-by-side on small landholdings (as had master and man). Now the field hands tended, increasingly, to be black and enslaved. The British, unlike the Spaniards and Portuguese, had no legal tradition of keeping slaves. And although they had dabbled in slavery, the British involvement in slavery had up to now been marginal. The truth of the matter was that in the shift to sugar, Barbadian landowners simply could not find enough pliant labour for their fields. A black slave, tied to the land in perpetuity, made better financial sense than the relatively expensive investment in indentured labour – which in any case was freed (and looking for land of its own) at the end of a finite indenture (R. S. Dunn, 1972, 71–2).

British ownership of Barbados was crucial for the broader history of British overseas history. First of all it firmly

B

established sugar as the most important, the most lucrative and most popular tropical staple, demand for which seemed insatiable by the mid-seventeenth century. It underlined what had already been proved by the Portuguese and Dutch in Brazil: African slaves offered the only viable labour force for sugar plantations as they were relatively cheap, easily replaced and to be found in abundance. And Barbados helped promote England as Europe's premier slave trader. A British slave trading company, with Royal backing and approval, vied with a growing army of English private traders to satisfy the burgeoning Caribbean demand for African slaves. Then, in 1672, the Royal African Company was formed and given a monopoly of English slave trading, and although it proved a commercial success it could never fully satisfy the voracious demand for slaves. Throughout its history, it was under pressure from a swarm of private interlopers. Despite costly punishments, the interlopers persisted, knowing that the demand for slaves offered an irresistible financial reward. By the early eighteenth century it was perfectly clear that free trade in slaves greatly benefited the planters and did little harm to England's overall trading position on the high seas or in Africa. An Act of 1712 conceded free trade, 'a Trade so very profitable in its selfe, and so absolutely necessary for the support of the plantations'. (J. Rawley, 1981, 162).

In the seventeenth century some 264,000 slaves were imported in the British islands, a substantial number coming initially from Dutch slave traders. By 1730, however, England had become the world's major slave trader. She was not dislodged until abolition of the slave trade in 1807. By the late eighteenth century the English were exporting 45,000 Africans per year. From 1690 to 1760 the English exported about 1,200,000 Africans; from then to 1810, some 1,613,000. Throughout its slave trading history, the British carried almost 3 million slaves from Africa into the New World.

The sharpest leap in British slave trading took place in the late seventeenth century. And the reason was simple: the development of Jamaica (and to a lesser extent the founding of the tobacco economy of the Chesapeake). Jamaica was seized from the Spaniards in 1655 as a consolation prize; Cromwell had instructed his invading army to take Hispaniola. But this luxuriant afterthought quickly proved itself to be invaluable. Much bigger than Barbados – twenty-six times bigger – (though mountainous and inaccessible along its spine), the island offered great expanses of coastal plains and inland valleys ideally suited to sugar cultivation. The soldiers who became the first generation of planters had the previous experience of Barbados to draw upon; there was also backing in abundance for the costly investments in plant, equipment – and slaves. By 1680 more than a third of all British slaves went to Jamaica, and throughout its slave history the island soaked up the largest proportion of Africans exported to the British West Indies.

For the first century of Jamaica's modern history, the island seemed never able to get all the slaves it wanted. But it witnessed an extraordinary growth nonetheless. On the eve of the American Revolution, Jamaica's slave population was almost 200,000 and there were perhaps 775 estates. By then, Jamaica had three times the number of slaves in Barbados and exported ten times the quantity of sugar. Jamaica's sugar revenue was worth £1·6 million a year with most estates turning in a handsome yearly profit. It was by far the most valuable of all British colonies in the Americas. Yet sugar did not dominate the island economy the way it did in the smaller British islands. Slaves worked in rum production, on their own provision grounds, with livestock and a string of other staples. And despite the predominance of black slaves, Jamaica continued to attract white immigrants from Britain, much like the colonies in North America.

In Jamaica the wealthiest planters formed the island's social and political elite, lording it above a middle class of white professionals, small planters and merchants, centring their dominance on the splendour of the capital Spanish Town. On their properties, they built the Great Houses as a grand statement of their wealth and status. But beneath all simmered a vast black labouring force, the bulk (until late in the history of slavery) imported Africans, aliens to the place, to the work − to the very language of their owners. Yet they were bowed to a lifetime's régime of work with little prospect of remission and unable to bestow on their offspring little but an inherited slavery. And since most of their lives were dominated by sugar, the working disciplines imposed on them were generally harsh and un-relenting. It is not surprising to learn that servile revolt was not only a permanent threat, but also a regular occurrence. Planters, especially those on remote and isolated properties, lived in permanent fear of slave uprising and violence (J. P. Greene, 1988, Ch. 7).

The boom in the British slave trade from the mid-seventeenth century was also greatly assisted by the growth of slavery in the colonies in North America. The boom years for North American slavery were the nine-teenth century when the new cotton regions of the South gave a remarkable filip to an institution which was, by then, in decline. But slavery was important in the earlier phase of colonial North American history. Slavery in Virginia, for instance, although established at an early date, was not significant for much of the seventeenth century. What was to change this pattern was, as in the West Indies, a major shift in the local economy. Sugar revolutionised the Caribbean; tobacco had a similar effect in Virginia.

Slaves were first landed in Virginia in 1617, but for much of the century the flow of slaves into the colony was minute. Why import slaves into Virginia when such good prices could be had in Barbados and then Jamaica? Imports were measured in their hundreds until 1660. But by 1700 there were more than 16,000 slaves in Virginia (about a quarter of the total population). By 1780 there were more than 220,000 slaves, some 41 per cent of the total population (C. Duncan Rice, 1975, 52; J. P. Greene, 1988). On the eve of the American Revolution, more than half of all the slaves in the Northern Colonies lived in Virginia or neighbouring Maryland (a ratio which continued long after independence).

The settlement of Virginia and the other Northern Colonies was not dependent on black slavery. But it did rely upon indentured white servitude. Poor whites from Britain indentured themselves for a given number of years, a pattern which had been common in Barbados in its early years before the sugar revolution. In Virginia, white servitude began to be displaced by black slavery after 1675, a period when the previously flagging tobacco industry went into an upward spiral of rising prices, vast overseas sales and a growing demand for cheap, malleable and readily recruited labour. Yet the transition to slavery was not as dramatic as it had been in the Caribbean. Black slave and white indentured worker laboured side by side in the Virginian tobacco fields. But by 1710 the tobacco industry of the Chesapeake was wedded to slave labour.

South Carolina was soon won over to slavery. From the first the colony had close connections with the Caribbean, especially with Barbados. After 1690, rice – possibly introduced by the slaves themselves – became the basic staple (along with the naval stores found in the colony in

abundance). Beginning near Charleston, the rice plantations spread throughout the coastal low country, laying
the basis for the colony's prosperity – and the slaves'
misery. By 1720 slaves outnumbered whites by 2 to 1.
They worked at a task system (unlike the more oppressive
West Indian slave gang system) in a hostile physical
environment. Their efforts produced great bounty; by 1730
2 million pounds of rice were exported annually. By 1740
South Carolina was home to 40,000 slaves, though most
of them were owned in small handfuls of three or four.
Slaves on the bigger West Indian plantations, however,
were owned in their hundreds. In Charleston and elsewhere
planters developed a lavish lifestyle which confirmed
the remarkable fortunes to be made from slave-grown
produce.

   In the northern colonies, slavery was able to establish
itself, again as in the West Indies, because its economic
attractions were so obvious and so clearly superior to the
alternatives. Slaves posed their own problems, but so too
had indentured workers who, once freed, tended to make
demands on the land or became discontented and politically
troublesome. There were rebellions (Bacon's rebellion
1675–6, the Protestant Rebellion in Maryland, 1688) which
were fuelled in part by the grievances of young white
working men. By 1690 the fear of white lower class revolt
had been replaced by the fear of slave revolt (J.P. Greene,
1988, 83). And as the blacks increased in number, their
status, treatment and legal position deteriorated markedly. As tobacco and rice became the major industries,
employing a primarily black enslaved labour force, local
society, like that throughout the British West Indian
islands, became a caste society. At its base lay a large
and growing black class, viewed and treated as unalterably
inferior and removed in most key respects in the eyes of

their white superiors from the world of humanity. Slaves in South Carolina and Virginia, like their cousins in the West Indies, were now things: items of trade and the objects of material possession. By 1810, 376,500 Africans had been imported into British North America. However, this compares to the 1,361,800 imported into the British West Indies (into a region which was very much smaller in land area) (J. Rawley, 1981, 167). These are vast numbers, and the arguments among historians about their exact precision can never hide the enormity of the phenomenon, nor its painful impact on the millions of Africans involved.

The vital influence of slavery on the colonies was obvious enough. The slave colonies became a byword for wealth, extravagance and commercial opportunities. But the fruits of slavery could not be measured solely in such beneficial terms. The slave colonies were renowned for their appalling death rates (both black and white – though it was generally only white mortality which caught the eye). They were home to a host of tropical ailments, where death and illness struck suddenly and without warning. The Atlantic slave system formed a fertile breeding ground for the diseases of three continents. Europeans died on the African coast, Africans died on board the slave ships and soon after arrival in the plantations. And native American peoples everywhere succumbed to a range of imported ailments. The slave colonies also became infamous for their savagery: for the physical pain and threats apparently necessary to keep the slave force in its place and at its duties, as well as the terrible penalties the slaves occasionally exacted of their masters and mistresses in regular and periodic rebellions and casual acts of violence. Whatever wealth might accrue to those involved in the business of slavery – sailors on the slave ships, or planters and managers on the plantations – a good case could be made that they deserved every

[31]

penny. Of course, those who also deserved some return for their efforts – the slaves themselves – got naught for their labours.

The British slave system which evolved in the Americas owed, as we have seen, a great deal to earlier European pioneers: to the Portuguese, the Spaniards and the Dutch. But it was a system which, notwithstanding the differences between one colony and another, and between one side of the Atlantic and the other, depended on much more than the accidents of history or the contingent forces of economic changes. Slavery was, from the first, a system which was closely regulated and shaped by the process of law.

The British settlers in the Americas, unlike the Spaniards, had no legal tradition of slavery to fall back on or to incorporate into their American ventures. But slavery was a legal entity as much as an economic institution. In the purchasing, shipping and daily regulation of slaves, a complex legal process evolved which ensured that the slave was more than a mere item of trade; he or she was given a legal status which itself had a host of ramifications on both sides of the Atlantic.

Settlers throughout the New World had to create a new society. Once the basic needs of survival were settled, the political, legal and administrative structure necessary to a civilised society emerged. And settlers were often conscious of the need to create the full structure of a civilisation, perched as they were precariously on an unknown word, often hemmed in by 'savages' (the local Indians) and harbouring growing numbers of alien peoples from Africa. Thus the slave laws devised by Europeans in the Americas were only one aspect of a wider legal framework designed to give their world a civility and structure.

In the West Indies, as the slaves began to outnumber the whites, it was imperative to devise laws to control the slaves. The guiding principle governing slave laws was simple enough. In the words of one commentator (describing West Indian slave laws in 1789): 'The leading Idea in the Negro System of Jurisprudence is that, which was the first in the Minds of those most interested in its Formation; namely, that Negroes were property, and a Species of Property that needed a rigorous and vigilant Regulation.' (M. Craton *et al.*, 1976, 181.) In Barbados, laws governing the slaves were devised in the 1640s and 1650s; a more comprehensive slave law of 1664 was promptly copied by the Jamaicans in 1667 and thence passed to Antigua and South Carolina. The initially piecemeal laws were soon replaced by more codified laws, but all were designed to control the slaves. A Barbadian Act of 1688 stated: 'forasmuch as the said Negroes and other Slaves brought into the People of this Island ... are of Barbarous, wild and savage Natures, and such renders them wholly unqualified to be governed by the Laws, Customs and Practices of our Nation.' (C. Duncan Rice, 1975, 68.)

Slave laws varied from colony to colony and although many were draconian, it is often difficult to tell how rigorously such laws were enforced. The most severe measures were designed to punish slave revolt and resistance; for acts of black violence, the local laws demanded – and got – revenge of excruciating cruelty.

There were, from the first, a number of contradictions in the laws governing slaves. How could a slave – a thing – be responsible for his/her own actions? Moral responsibility rested uneasily with the chattel status of the slaves. The simple truth of the matter was that most slaves were governed, not so much by the local legal system, as by their owners and masters. And in remoter rural communities, the control of the masters was absolute and generally unquestioned.

Planters in the main felt secure in whatever punishments they meted out to their slaves. In many colonies they *were* the law: the law makers and enforcers. Indeed, the very structure of law was designed to make safe and efficient the planter's world. Slaves were not allowed to 'wander'. Slave property could be searched and confiscated. Slave violence – or hints of violence – were punished by beatings, mutilations or death. Captors of runaways were rewarded. These clauses and more were fashioned initially by Barbadian planter/legislators. By the end of the seventeenth century variations on such legal formulations were to be found throughout the British colonies. And with each major slave revolt, penalties against the slaves grew more severe. The slave was effectively denied any rights and was left at the mercy, not only of his master, but of the white community as a whole.

It would be wrong to imagine that the British legal definition of slavery evolved solely from colonial experience. From an early date the British devised a series of Acts, and made a number of legal judgements or opinions, which confirmed the status of the slave as a thing, as an inanimate piece of property, a chattel. This represented a major change in experience and practice, for English law had no basis for treating people as chattels since the decline of feudalism.

Anglo-Saxon England had been a slave-owning society. Even after the Norman Conquest, a large servile population remained basic to English society. In the Domesday Book, for instance, slaves comprised between 9 and 20 per cent of the population. Serfdom – different from slavery but less than freedom – had, however, effectively died out in England by the time the English had begun to acquire their possessions in the New World. Indeed, in the very years the English settled the Americas they were proudly insistent that freedom, not slavery, was the basic characteristic of

English life: 'As for slaves and bondsmen we have none; nay
such is the privilege of our country by the special grace of
God and bounty of our princes, that if any came hither from
other realms, as soon as they set foot on land they become
free ... all note of servile bondage is utterly removed from
them.' (R. Hilton, 1969, 56.)

In the middle years of the seventeenth century, as the
British settled their American colonies, the Revolution at
home spawned a fierce debate about liberties and slavery.
It was widely argued that slavery was the worst condition
known to man. Yet this was the historical moment when
the British began to impose slavery on growing numbers
of Africans. As the Africans poured into the colonies, the
status of the early indentured white settlers rose. The law,
in London and in colonial capitals, transformed the black
into a thing, 'to be bought and sold, a status applicable
only and necessarily to blacks and to their descendants'
(J. Walvin, 1986, 29).

The slave was defined by the law as a thing long before
he or she was landed in America. Like the other European
slave trading nations, the British tried initially to organise
their Atlantic trade through a monopoly company, the
Royal African Company (founded in 1672). But in the debate
about how that trade should be organised, slavery – the
central issue – was a matter of political debate in England
itself. Thus, slavery was a major political question in
domestic politics; it was not an institution quietly consigned to the distant peripheries of colonial life. Navigation
Acts, passed by Parliament, regulated conditions on the
slave trade. Acts from Colonial Assemblies came to London
for approval or alteration.

English slave law was complex, however. There were
sometimes disputes between the different sections of the
slave empire (laws thought too severe in London looked

[35]

perfectly unexceptional in Bridgetown or Kingston). And the legal problems were amply illustrated when English courts had to deal with the question of slavery in England itself. If slaves could be legally held on the far side of the Atlantic, why could they not be held in England or, under a separate legal system, in Scotland? This problem worsened as more slaves settled in England, the possessions of returning sailors and colonial officials, or having merely been bought in coffee shops and auction rooms in London, Bristol or Liverpool.

From the early seventeenth century a noticeable (though always small) black population developed in England, mainly in the capital (the nation's major seaport). Many of these blacks had been imported as slaves. Sometimes they – or their friends – challenged their status as slaves in the courts. And from the mid-seventeenth century to the ending of slavery itself, English courts had to deal with the various problems created by trying to maintain slavery in what was essentially a free land.

There was a host of legal decisions, some of them contradictory, some of them misunderstood in retrospect, trying to resolve the question of whether slavery was legal in England (or Scotland) as opposed to in the colonies. Whatever the latest legal judgement, slaves continued to be imported into England, in small numbers admittedly, working mainly as domestics, but many of them settling down as free people in London. As the slave empire of the Americas grew, it was inevitable that more and more blacks would find their way to England to form the nucleus of the first major black population in English history. Reminders of their presence, especially in the mid to late eighteenth century, can still be seen in contemporary cartoons, portraits and descriptions of social life. Many ran away from their owners/employers, and advertisements for them (or offering others for sale) were common in eighteenth-century newspapers.

While the history of black society in England itself is a minor aspect of the broader history of slaves, it provides a revealing insight into the English involvement with slavery. It needs to be stressed that slavery and the slave trade were not matters of distant or marginal importance. They had a number of direct consequences for domestic life. Clearly, the wealth accruing to the homeland was of great importance, as was the legal debate about slavery. And no less telling was the settlement of a black community in England: a human reminder of the even greater black communities on the far side of the Atlantic whose labours were so vital to the material well-being of the Empire.

The Enigsh were in no doubt that slavery was a source of great prosperity to themselves. It was a matter of popular debate that the West Indies – whatever mortal dangers might threaten the white settlers – generated exceptional wealth for those who persevered and survived. Returning planters, awash with ostentatious wealth from the Indies, were the objects of jokes in eighteenth-century cartoons, writings and social commentary. Even the King made remarks at their expense. And for those who needed convincing of the importance of slavery and the slave trade, a visit to England's major ports would have resolved any lingering doubts.

The slave trade created wealth and diverse economic activity in those major ports which serviced the Atlantic trade. There was a host of small ports whose ships carried slaves across the Atlantic. Ships left Lancaster, Preston, Glasgow, Plymouth, Whitehaven, Dartmouth, Cowes, Portsmouth, Poole and Southampton for the slave baracoons of Africa and the voyage to America (N. Tattersfield, 1991). But the bulk of the trade – and the surviving popular imagery of the slave trade – was firmly the preserve of Bristol, London and Liverpool.

When Britain gained the upper hand in the international slave trade, it did so through London, where the existing shipping and trading houses – sources of capital and goods coupled with political and royal support – provided the necessary infrastructure for the trade to Africa and the Americas. With the trade organised under the monopoly of the Royal African Company, there developed the 'triangular trade', with ships clearing from London, trading goods (from Britain, Europe and Asia) at a number of chosen spots in West Africa for slaves, who were then shipped into the West Indies. From there, tropical produce was shipped back to Britain (extra ships were often hired for the leg back to carry the bulkier goods, notably the sugar and rum).

Once the monopoly of the Royal African Company had been broken (it was, from the first, under threat from inter-lopers always able to make money from slave-hungry planters) the slave trade boomed as never before. And as a freer trade in slaves developed, so too did the fortunes of the newer slave ports, notably Bristol and later Liverpool and the smaller ports.

Bristol began to outstrip London as a slaving port in the early eighteenth century. It was, said Daniel Defoe, 'the greatest, the richest, and the best Port of Trade in Great Britain, London only excepted'. The West Indies became the backbone of Bristol's trade; a flow of goods from the city's hinterland was fed onwards to Africa, and the produce of the Indies were refined and marketed through Bristol. The city's leading merchants and politicians were promi-nent Bristol's maritime interests (and were, in the late eighteenth century, the most resistant of opponents of the abolition movement). The slave traders and merchants of Bristol dominated and dictated the social style of the city;

they built splendid shipping and storage facilities, and lavished much of their spare cash on the elaborate homes and social lives which characterised the style of those involved in slavery on both sides of the Atlantic.

Bristol merchants established their agents on both sides of the Atlantic and had business contacts throughout the American colonies. They each had their favourite, well-established point in Africa for bartering for slaves. And similarly they had well-tried outlets for their slaves in America. But they were sufficiently flexible to shift their points of sale as the American markets shifted. The end result was not only the personal advancement of the Bristol merchants, but the rapid growth of Bristol itself. It became, like Bordeaux and Nantes, an elegant and prosperous example of the fruits of the slave trade.

When the English slave trade reached its apogee from the mid-eighteenth century onwards, the main slave port was Liverpool. Long before the 'industrial revolution', Liverpool had established itself as a growing Atlantic port. Agents from Liverpool were active in Virginia and then in the West Indies, and the trade they generated was accelerated by the money invested in the city's trade by local landowners. A thriving merchant community grew in Liverpool, and its members collectively realised the profits that were to be from the slave trade. Perhaps the most famous was Gladstone's father, whose family fortunes rested securely on business transactions in the West Indies (S. O. and E. A. O. Checkland, 1974).

Profits from the trade were invested both in the growth of the Liverpool fleet and in the expansion of the city's port facilities. In their turn these greatly encouraged the growth of local banking and financial services. Yet even at its peak, Liverpool's slave trading took up no more than 20 per cent of the city's maritime trade (R. Anstey, 1975; Solow and

Engerman, 1988). Of course, Liverpool interests soon became vocal in London's corridors of power. And the city's merchants and political spokesmen led the rearguard campaign against the attacks of the abolitionists after 1787.

Liverpool's prominence in the campaign to maintain the slave trade after 1787 was natural enough, for by that time the city had become England's leading slave trader. In fact, Liverpool had established an early lead in the shipping of Africans as early as the 1740s and increased its share in the slave trade rapidly thereafter. Between 1750 and 1775, 1,868 ships left the city for Africa. By the early 1770s 67 per cent of England's slave trade was from Liverpool, increasing to 85 per cent by the end of the trade (J. Rawley, 1981, 206). As in Bristol, fortunes accrued to Liverpool and its slaving families. And, again as in Bristol, those family fortunes were often invested in splendid local buildings (many forgotten in the later transformation of Liverpool in the nineteenth century).

It was only one of many ironies of the history of slavery and the slave trade that the men who benefited so impressively from the slave trade were often the most vociferous in the defence of their own social and political liberties. Those involved in the slave trade defended their right to trade – for the benefit of the nation – wherever and however they could. The rights of free trade and commercial prosperity dictated the right to trade in humanity. The British had, since the early seventeenth century, been engaged in what, in retrospect, seems a tortuous (not to say contradictory) process of extolling their own liberties while making vast profits from the denial of the same liberties to others.

4

The slave trade

All the Africans deposited in the Americas had been human cargoes in the holds of the slave ships which crossed the Atlantic with growing frequency in the seventeenth and eighteenth centuries. As we have seen, the British were not the pioneers of the slave trade, but in the course of feeding their colonies in the West Indies and North America they became the world's leading trader in Africans. In the process they developed a complex and sophisticated trading system, linking Britain, West Africa and the Americas. But an even greater, global trade was drawn into the slave system. Textiles from India, cowrie shells from the Maldives (used as currency in West Africa), European wines and luxuries – all and more found themselves bought and bartered in the slave traders' business deals on both sides of the Atlantic.

As the slave trade grew in size, and as time progressed, the slave trade itself changed. The size of boats and the timing of the Atlantic crossing, for instance, changed quite markedly. The ships which traded to Africa in the early years of the English trade took a variety of commodities for barter and trade with African middlemen: metal and metal goods, woollens, textiles from India, gunpowder, knives, beads and cowrie shells, food from Ireland and Scotland. Slaves were bought or bartered on board an anchored ship or on shore. In some regions the British, like others before them, built major 'factories' or forts which they used as trading posts and as warehouses for slaves gathered from the interior (J. Rawley, 1981, 205).

When Bristol emerged as a major slaving port, products from local industries and from the East Indies and Manchester found their way to West Africa in return for slaves. When Liverpool's ships became the main slave traders, the trade relied largely on cotton and metal goods, manufactured throughout the Lancashire region, as the means of exchange. All the major ports re-exported a number of goods, from India and Europe, to West Africa. The slave traders were conscious of the preferences of the New World slave owners; they wanted by and large, healthy young males, and they often had pronounced views about the desirability (or otherwise) of certain tribal groups. Some were thought too troublesome or too warlike. Others were thought to be more docile and malleable. But the problem facing the slave traders was the simple matter of supply. The traders were at the mercy of the market in slaves which funnelled Africans to the slave sales on the coast. The slaves were produced by internal warfare and slave-raids; the prisoners of war, or the prisoners of slave-raiding parties, were then ferried along an increasingly complex internal slave trade. As demand for slaves grew, fuelled by the appetite of the colonies, the demand on the African coast could only be satisfied by deliberate slave trading in the interior. Often Africans caught in the outer edges of the slave-trading net spent many months travelling along pathways and especially river systems before they reached the open sea and were confronted for the first time by whites. It was a traumatic experience, even before reaching the Atlantic. What was to follow passed imagination.

By modern standards, the ships used in the Atlantic trade were extremely small. Although they increased in size as the slave trade progressed, they tended to be greater than

200 tons only by the last years of the slave trade. Of course, this was true of most merchant ships, which got bigger in the course of the eighteenth century. But the slave ships of the late seventeenth century, for instance, were often no more than 100 tons. The slave ships were often built locally, but from the mid-eighteenth century, with the massive expansion of the Liverpool trade, ships built in that city became more popular, even among slave traders in Bristol. But so expansive was the trade that slavers acquired their vessels from any possible source: as bounty, from the colonies, or from other parts of Britain. But the general rule seems to have been that as the slave trade progressed, the slave ships got bigger and heavier. By the last years of the trade, ships of more than 300 tons were common.

The nature of slave trading on the African coast depended greatly on the geography of the region. On those coastal stretches with no real or natural harbour facilities, the trading tended to take place off-shore. Small boats or canoes ferried batches of slaves to the English ships for barter and purchase. Elsewhere, trade was done on land in the major factories or forts. In other places, slaves were sold in makeshift arrangements, in tents or temporary huts. But in general, the process of selection and purchase tended to follow a pattern. The slaves were inspected for their condition by an experienced slave captain, often aided by his 'surgeon', both trying to select the Africans best able to survive the Atlantic crossing and likely then to fetch the best price in America. The slaves were 'sold in open Market on shore, and examined by us in like manner as our Brother Trade do Beasts in Smithfield; the Countenance, and Stature, a good set of teeth, Pliancy in the Limbs, and Joints, and being free of Veneral Taint ...' (M. Craton *et al.*, 1976, 33).

Often, however, the slave captains had little choice in

the matter; rarely were they able to gather a full cargo in one single operation. More likely, they had to ply up and down the coast, collecting a few slaves here and there, backtracking when they heard of others newly arrived somewhere close, buying a handful in one place and a few more at the next point. To make the frustration worse, it was well known that the longer a slave ship lingered on the coast seeking a full cargo of slaves, the more likely it was that white crew would die. West Africa was infamous for its mortality levels for whites who worked in or visited the region. The less time a slave ship spent on the coast, the happier the slave captain was. The slave ships rarely had a full complement of crew (slave ships had a reputation as the most awful of all maritime work), and to lose crewmen in West Africa could pare down the crew's complement to dangerous levels.

White sailors died in horrifying numbers. Africa was, from the early days of white exploration, known as the white man's graveyard. Those who worked ashore – for the slave trading companies – died at an alarming rate; three out of five died within the first year. It has been claimed that no more than 10 per cent actually returned to England (S.L. Engerman and E.D. Genovese, 1974). Of course, maritime trade was always a high-risk venture and sudden or catastrophic loss of life was common. But it was dramatically worse on the slave ships. Perhaps a quarter of all sailors involved died, and the story was repeated, with local variations, wherever Europeans plied their trade to and from West Africa.

It is now thought that white sailors were much more likely to die on the Middle Passage than the slaves; the proportion of white deaths was upwards of twice that of slave deaths. Of course we need to stress that the numbers were greatly different; there were vastly more slaves

involved than white sailors. And it also needs to be said
that Europeans were sailing in an utterly alien disease environment, exposed to diseases and complaints to which
they had no or little resistance or immunity. For the slaves,
death and disease stalked the slave ships and the slave
baracoons on the coast. What determined the levels of slave
deaths were the conditions on the ships and the conditions
in Africa itself.

As the eighteenth century advanced, the death rate
among the slaves on board the slavers declined. It tended
to vary between the different nations, but it now seems
clear that the losses of slaves were not as high as many
initially claimed; often the percentage loss was in double
figures, but it dropped into single figures as the century
advanced.

Slaves were traumatised by being thrust into the bowels
of the slave ships. Many slipped into a gloom which hastened the advance of more physical ailments. Many were swept
away by disease which found a fertile breeding ground in
the squalid and cramped ship's environment. Dysentery
was particularly rife and lethal, carried by polluted water
and the stable-like filth. Generally, the slaves' ailments on
shipboard were beyond medical help, although well-tried
medical customs developed and slave captains made great
efforts to save their slaves. Slavers carried doctors (or men
described as doctors) and an array of medicines. After all,
dead or diseased slaves were a financial loss for the venture.
It was appreciated that cleanliness was important, but in
the human squalor of an Atlantic crossing, especially a
rough crossing, when all hands were busy sailing the ship
with little time for the care of the slaves, the ideal treatment
of the human cargoes simply degenerated into a disgusting
and often fatal neglect. The sick and the healthy, the living
and the dead remained shackled for days on end, unfed,

[45]

unwashed and unexercised, as their vessel rode out an Atlantic storm.

The males were shackled together. Slave traders could never escape the fear – and sometimes the reality – of slave revolts on board. Women and children, kept separately, remained exposed to sexual abuse from the crew. As in most aspects of the voyage, their fate depended to a large extent on the captain: on his régime and his determination to maintain a clean and disciplined vessel. But even the best of captains could not escape the vagaries of the weather and the accidents of life at sea.

However much a slave captain might try to keep his human cargo in reasonable health, there were limits to what he could do to shield his slaves from the ravages of disease or the unwelcome assaults of sailors. And if a crossing was especially stormy and therefore prolonged, the ship's supplies, always carefully calculated and stored in the knowledge of how long the voyage would last, could run low – or even run out. When a slaver crossed the Atlantic, it was even more precarious a venture than the normal transatlantic voyage.

White crews were themselves at risk, not simply from the diseases of Africa or from contagion on the high seas, but especially from slave revolts. Slaves often tried to fight back: to revolt or simply to harm the whites who had inflicted such sufferings on them. Time and again, slave captains described nipping rebellion in the bud. John Newton, later to be a leading abolitionist, was a successful slave trade captain. In 1752 he discovered a slave revolt on his ship.

By the favour of Divine Providence made a timely discovery today that the slaves were forming a plot for an insurrection. Surprised two of them attempting to get off their irons, and upon further search in their rooms,

upon the information of three of the boys, found some
knives, stones, shot, etc. ... and a cold chisel ... Put
the boys in irons and slightly in the thumbscrews to urge
them to a full confession ... (J. Newton (1788), 1962.)

Sometimes such rebellions were successful, but by and
large the crews were able to maintain their control.
Needless to say, slaves who tried to resist were punished
savagely. This was to be a familiar pattern in the slave communities in America; endemic black resistance prompted
the most savage of white reprisals.

Slave resistance on the ships sometimes took another
bleak form. It was common for slaves, despairing of their
fate, to fling themselves overboard and drown. The crew
took precautions to stop it, but whenever the opportunity
arose there was always the possibility that some slaves
would commit suicide at sea. Equiano, a former slave whose
autobiography provides an invaluable insight into the
experience on board a slave ship, witnessed one such inci-
dent: 'two of my wearied countrymen who were chained
together ... preferred death to such a life of misery, some-
how made through the nettings and jumped into the sea.'
(P. Edwards, 1970, 29.)

It is natural enough to think of the slave traders as wicked
and cruel men, yet they had a vested interest in caring for
their slaves. It was in their economic interests to maintain
a healthy slave cargo until they reached the markets of the
Americas. Obviously, there was individual cruelty in abundance (John Newton did not think it at all cruel to put slaves
in thumbscrews) – to say nothing of the cruelty inherent
in the whole system, yet there was a powerful economic
incentive for the slavers to look after their slaves as best
they could. The slave trade came to be governed, in theory
at least, by a series of precepts, often printed in manuals
carried on board the ships, telling how best to care for slaves:

how to feed, clothe, nurse and house them. Like all printed treatises there tended to be a gulf between social reality as it unfolded between decks on the slave ships and the ideal system described in the manuals. There were supposed to be well-established routines for caring for the slaves once they came on board: for cleaning the ships and providing the slaves with a decent food and regular exercise. It was widely known that a successful trip depended largely upon 'the wholesome Victualling, and Management of Slaves on Board'. Slaves, in such an ideal regime, had regular ablutions, had their mouths washed with vinegar or lime, were given foods they liked and fresh water to drink. We can only guess at how often this ideal came close to reality.

Among the more persistent of popular images of the slave trade is the picture of slaves packed head to toe: human sardines in a pestilential hold. In fact, as the slave trade grew in size, the 'packing' of slaves improved (i.e. slaves were less densely crowded into the holds than had been the pattern in the early years). The slave traders themselves realised, from an early date, that it made poor commercial sense to pack slaves indiscriminately into their holds. By the mid-seventeenth century, slave traders frequently commented on overcrowding as a major factor in slave mortality on the Atlantic crossing. Yet it remains unclear the extent to which overcrowding really was a major cause of increased slave mortality. What determined the levels of deaths among the slaves was the time it took to cross the ocean: the longer the voyage, the higher the death rate. Equally, the longer a ship lingered on the African coast, the higher the slave death rate (H. Klein, 1986).

Despite these factors, it is also true that slave mortality declined as the eighteenth century advanced – as the British slave trade reached its peak. To a marked degree that was the result of experience. As with any commercial venture, the simple fact that the British had accumulated a century's experience of slave trading enabled them to improve their performance – in this case to reduce the levels of slave deaths on the ships. The ships themselves were better: custom-built to carry slaves, and faster on the Atlantic crossing.

Above all else perhaps was the economic impulse. It was to everyone's commercial benefit to keep the slaves alive and well. By the time the British Parliament insisted on better shipping conditions for slaves (in 1788), such improvements had already begun to make themselves felt. Slaves benefited in the sense that the slave trade was economically more efficient. They would have benefited even more had it not existed.

When ready for the crossing, the slave ships headed west into the Atlantic on a voyage that took up to three or four months. The pattern for the British voyages was well established. Landfall in Barbados, the Leeward Islands and thence to Jamaica and, sometimes, onwards to the North American colonies. Large numbers of slaves were trans-shipped at the ports of the British Caribbean: in Bridgetown, Basseterre, St John, Kingston, and from Charleston. From about 1740 onwards, Rhode Island became the centre for slaves landing in North America. What happened to the Africans on arrival was but another chapter in the continuing saga of their imiseration.

Slave traders took particular care to ensure that their human cargoes were in a presentable condition before they were sold. Often, a company or a planter's agent had ordered certain numbers of slaves. But the physical condition of the slaves (and their age and sex) were crucial in determining the price they would fetch. The slaves were cleaned and shaved, sometimes oiled to mask their pallor with a sheen, sometimes bunged up to hide their dysentery. Grey hair was dyed black. And then the factors and agents were allowed on board to make a preliminary inspection. Notices were published advertising the slave sale at the appointed time. Sometimes, the sale took place on board the ship. At other times the slaves were sold, like other commodities, in more public places ashore. The sales were often protracted, the best slaves obviously going first and fetching the best prices. The old, the weak or the sick were harder to sell and were generally described as 'refuse slaves'. In the West Indies, the slaves were often trans-shipped and possibly sold again, to planters in the smaller islands. In fact slaves throughout the Americas were sold and re-sold. Slaves sold in the West Indies were brought to the Northern Colonies and paraded up and down the Chesapeake river system before finding a final owner. But even then, they might face further sales, into the interior, as middlemen passed them on to settlements away from the coast (A. Kulikoff, 1986, 322–3).

In the West Indies, new arrivals were sometimes sold through a 'scramble', when, at a given signal, prospective buyers rushed towards the slaves, physically grabbing and claiming those they wanted to buy. The effect of these bizarre happenings on the slaves (already traumatised by the sea crossing) can readily be imagined. But their misfortunes were not yet over. The slaves, once purchased in the colonies, began the often long trek to their new homes. Leaving behind the friends they had made on board the slaver (generally the most significant associates in their lives thereafter), the slaves set off on foot, in small bands or individually, towards their new homes.

Even before the new arrivals began their life as slaves, they faced a series of major problems. Many of them simply did not acclimatise to their new environment. Many arrived sick, having brought ailments from Africa, or, as likely, having contracted illnesses or weaknesses on board the slave ship. In the West Indies it was the practice for planters to put their new slaves through a 'seasoning process', placing them, if possible, in less arduous work, for up to two years until they had shaken off the infirmities and disturbances of the Atlantic crossing. Many slaves were so sick after the journey that they simply could not work. Among those sold into the Chesapeake in the early eighteenth century, one in four died in their first year. It was much the same story in the Caribbean where upwards of 25 per cent of the Africans could be expected to die within their first three years. Whenever a sugar estate bought a substantial batch of new slaves, the death rate among its slaves rose accordingly. Not only did the new slaves die in frightening numbers, but they often intruded contagious diseases among the established slaves on the estate.

The irony was that the more Africans were brought and introduced on to an estate, the higher the death rate, and the greater the need for more slaves to top-up the overall population. There were, of course, enormous variations in mortality rates among the slaves. But it was common throughout the slave colonies that sick and debilitated slaves, fresh from the slave ships, brought serious threats of ill health not just for themselves, but for those other slaves alongside whom they were forced to live and work.

The Atlantic slave trade was responsible for the removal of millions of Africans from their homelands and their enforced resettlement in alien lands. Africans and their descendants were to be found throughout the Americas by the mid-seventeenth century. But with the sugar and then the tobacco revolutions in Brazil, the West Indies and Virginia, an increasing concentration of those slaves found their way into those colonies undergoing massive economic growth. It seems in retrospect a bizarre economic formula:

wrenching millions of Africans from their homes (which were increasingly to be found away from the African coast) to transport them under the most abject of conditions, thousands of miles, to produce luxury goods to satisfy the tastes and fill the pockets of European consumers and investors. It seemed as if the demand for labour in the American colonies was inexhaustible; it also seemed that the ability of black Africa to satisfy that demand was equally inexhaustible. As the Indian populations of the Americas were decimated (and worse), the Africans arrived in ever greater numbers to take their place.

The slave trade has come to occupy a special but malignant place in popular imagination. In part this is because the images left by the trade remain so vivid. There is a host of visual evidence which speaks of the horrors of the trade. And there was a great deal of propaganda, generated mainly by abolitionists after 1787, and aimed at Parliament and the public, describing in terrible detail the full horrors of the slave trade. Much of that propaganda – like all forms of propaganda – tended to exaggerate or varnish the truth in order to undermine the slave trade by appalling the reader or the listener. Yet the truth of the slave trade is much more appalling than any propaganda could ever hope to be. The slave trade was one of those historical phenomena – not unlike the Holocaust – which is extremely difficult to describe in its full enormity. How to capture the sufferings of the millions of Africans caught in its pernicious web has eluded most historians. We can leave the matter hoping that the stark facts of the slave trade tell their own story.

5

Slaves at work

Work was the sole justification for importing Africans into
the colonies. Without the demand for their labours there
would have been no reason to transport them. Initially,
Africans were imported to be the beasts of burden: the men
and women who broke open the land to new tropical production and settlement. In time, however, slaves were to
be found in almost every conceivable occupation, from the
most brutish of labourers to the highly skilled artisans of
a mature economy.

In the early years of settlement, black and white worked
side by side in the demanding task of opening up virgin
land: cutting back the bush, building homes and clearing
fields and roads. What often made slave work worse – or
better – than the work of other men were the geophysical
conditions in which tropical staples thrived. It was into
the hotter regions that most of the Africans were taken
(providing the retrospective justification for black slavery
that Africans were accustomed to hot climates). As the
colonies became more temperate, slaves became fewer.
And in the hotter slave colonies, blacks soon greatly outnumbered local whites.

Slave owners were generally agreed that it was essential
to keep slaves busy. With the establishment of the major
tropical crops, notably sugar, rice and tobacco, this was
relatively easy for part of the year. In sugar, the cultivation
and processing of the cane imposed its own regime of work.

[53]

For six days a week slaves worked in gangs from dawn to
dusk, generally with an hour for lunch. But out of crop
time, work had sometimes to be invented. The slave gangs
were built up with an eye to their maximum use in crop
time. What to do with them for the rest of the year was a
permanent problem for slave owners.

Sugar slaves were organised in gangs; the 'Great Gang'
which did the back-breaking work, the 'Second Gang' for
the less demanding tasks, and then the 'weeding gang'. It
was through these gangs that slaves were taught their work
discipline – itself quite different from anything they might
have encountered in their African homelands. The gangs
were often large; as sugar expanded the plantations grew in
size, and so too did the labour force. In the sugar fields,
hundreds of slaves worked together, often far removed from
their white owners (who were invariably greatly outnumbered on the plantations). In North America, slaves were
employed in much smaller groups, generally working closely with whites, from whom they learned a new language
and European social habits. Until the end of slavery, slaves
in the West Indies were much more African than their
cousins in the Northern Colonies, who at an earlier date
were socialised to white patterns more quickly. Slaves in
mid-eighteenth-century Chesapeake had become African-
Americans: English speakers and Christians with social
patterns which were quite different from those of West
Indian slaves.

The nature of slave work varied enormously, depending
in the main on the nature of the local crop. In South
Carolina, for instance, the slaves converted the swamps
and marshlands into fertile rice fields. It was regular, tiring
and often dangerous work. But in this case it seems that
some of the slaves' African work patterns and experience
was put to good use in the production process (C. Joyner,

1984; P. Wood, 1975). There, and throughout the slave colonies, slaves were kept at work by a combination of inducements and punishments. The threat of a beating was never far away. But punishment alone could not have kept the slaves at their tasks. Slave-owners generally offered their slaves rewards and incentives, often of the most basic kind (a little extra food, an extra day of rest, some more clothing).

Africans from the slave ships had to be broken into their new work patterns. Their local-born offspring did not pose the same problems for management, for they were born into slave society and were, from their earliest days, trained in the routines and habits of regular application and labour. The Africans, however, had to be taught. 'Breaking in' the slaves was a ritual of all slave societies: 'A new Negro, if he must be broke, will require more hard Discipline than a young Spaniel.' (A. Kulikoff, 1986, 382–3.)

Slave-owners throughout the Americas assumed that Africans were lazy. This was part of their justification – to themselves and outsiders – that slavery alone could persuade the slaves to work. Slavery was often justified in terms of it being the only way known to get the African and his descendants to labour effectively. Thus, black indolence and white discipline were two sides of the same ideological coin.

In some cases, African labour systems and skills were utilised by the slave-owners; this was notably the case with South Carolina rice cultivation. But the work rhythms which emerged among slaves in Africa were new: a mixture of traditional European patterns and the more tightly-disciplined routines of industrial society. Slaves were in effect trained in an industrial labour discipline long before the emergent European working class itself was. This was especially true in the sugar industry where work in the fields had to be carefully dovetailed to the mechanical rhythms of the factory and distillery where the sugar cane was processed. But to effect this discipline among their slaves, slave-owners had to impose an artificial and severe work discipline. 'I find it almost impossible to make a negro do his work well. No orders can engage it, no encouragement persuade it, nor no punishment oblige it' (E.D. Genovese, 1975, 299:) thus wrote a Virginia tobacco planter in 1772. Slavery was responsible for the spread of the myth of the lazy black; without the constraints of slavery, it was argued, the black would revert to his natural indolence.

Whatever the crop – sugar, rice or tobacco – the slave-owner or his agents were never far away to give a blow or a whipping. Of course, corporal punishment was commonplace throughout western society in those years. Beating children, for instance, was thought perfectly normal: a natural way of child-rearing. But the beating of slaves was different. For them, physical punishment was an inescapable aspect of their working lives. Beatings were doled out to discipline them, to punish and cajole and for a range of transgressions. They might be especially persecuted if owned or worked by a particularly vicious owner or employer. Slave-drivers in the Caribbean often carried whips, and there are many illustrations of slaves carrying the scars of their ill-treatment for the rest of their lives. But the more severe forms of such punishments were actively discouraged by the late eighteenth century for a variety of reasons. Some felt that it was economically counter-productive; it was also bad publicity for a slave regime which, after 1787, needed all the public support it could muster. But the truth of the matter was that whipping and slavery were indispensable bed-fellows. When enlightened owners tried to dispense with whippings they were often disappointed. By removing it, they discovered that 'we take away the motive that leads to labour on the neighbouring estates; that is, the dread of the lash' (R. Sheridan, 1985, 182).

Slavery changed as the slave economies changed. The frontier societies, in the islands and on the mainland, gave way to more sophisticated and mature societies whose produce was dispatched to Europe. And as the local economies became more mature, slavery itself became more diverse. Slave élites developed which do not easily fit the popular image of the brutalised field hand. Bigger slave holdings employed drivers and head slaves, domestics and nurses, factory craftsmen, coopers and carpenters for the barrels and woodwork, masons for building and repair work, smiths for the host of metalwork in and around the factories and houses. There were slaves employed as skilled herdsmen and cowboys, slaves who were sailors or river pilots, literate slaves, and many more besides. It is true that the largest single group were the slaves to be found bending their backs in the fields, but the slave societies could not have functioned without that array of skills to be found among the slaves. As in Europe, many of those skills were passed from father to son, mother to daughter. And with the skills went a superior status and preferential treatment.

Female slaves found it more difficult than males to secure skilled posts. They were worked, increasingly, in the fields or in domestic work. Both in the sugar fields, and later in the United States cotton fields, women came to predominate while their menfolk dominated the skilled occupations. Some skills were imported from Africa, for example, metalwork, the making of tools, woodwork, the making of clothes and cooking were clearly African-based skills to be found in slave societies. But most skilled slaves were trained by their masters (or people working for the owners). It is often forgotten that those monuments to the wealth

[57]

C

generated by slavery, especially the splendid Great Houses, the homes and furnishings of slave societies (notably in the American South), are as much a reflection of slave skills as of slave-owners' wealth. Without the strength and the skills of slaves, the material culture of slave society could not have come into being. We often lose sight of the skilled slaves, hidden by the imagery (itself real enough) of slaves at work in the cotton, rice or sugar fields.

Another group of slaves we tend to lose sight of are those involved in shipping. The coastal and river systems of the American colonies and that myriad of islands which form the West Indies were alive with boats of all sorts and conditions. Black crew, sailors and navigators were ubiquitous. Late-eighteenth-century prints and cartoons frequently portray blacks employed as sailors on British ships; many of them were slaves. Ferries and ocean-going vessels were often manned by slaves. In 1815 a slave-owner in Antigua offered for sale 'a stout negro man, a good sailor and fisherman, capable of taking charge of a vessel, and a good pilot for this and all the neighbouring islands' (B. Higman, 1984, 175). Slave fishermen were common throughout the smaller islands of the Caribbean, and throughout West Indian ports slaves were listed as sailors.

Africans were imported primarily to work in the fields, and planters preferred young men to women. But, as we have seen, by the late eighteenth century women were the dominant group in the cane fields as they were to be in the Southern cotton fields. As the slave societies matured and towns and small cities emerged, often from the initial port facilities, these urban areas became home to growing numbers of slaves. We tend, again, to think of slavery as a rural phenomenon: to imagine, perhaps, that slavery was inappropriate in an urban setting. Naturally enough, slaves in towns did not fit the patterns of their country-based cousins. By the end of slavery in the Caribbean perhaps 10 per cent of all slaves lived in towns. There, in contrast to life on the plantations, the slaves were greatly outnumbered by the whites. Many of them were women working as enslaved domestics, cooks or seamstresses. Many were skilled men: carpenters, masons, tailors, bakers, fishermen and hawkers. They enjoyed a level of economic and social independence unknown among slaves in the country. In the United States a smaller proportion of slaves lived in towns in the South, yet slaves could be found throughout urban North America. Both in North America and the West Indies it is not the case that urban life was inimical to slavery. Certainly, slavery was different in towns than in the country. Local laws tried to restrict the lives and movements of the slaves but these were rarely successful, and urban slaves tended to enjoy a greater freedom of movement and flexibility in their lives than slaves on the plantations.

As the slave-based economy matured, there was a noticeable shift in attitudes towards the kind of work black and white ought to do (or not to do). We have seen how, in the early days of settlement, black and white often worked side by side in the fields. This continued to be the case wherever slaves were owned or worked in small numbers; owners of a handful of slaves could often be found working with them. But where slave holdings became sizeable, and where white people tended to gravitate towards the managerial or supervisory roles, it came to be accepted that certain jobs were for blacks only. And one consequence of this was that slavery came to define what sort of work was inappropriate for white people. Whites were driven out of the fields by slavery. And, notwithstanding a host of exceptions, field labour came to be viewed as beneath the racial dignity of the humblest of white workers. Whites were reluctant to work at slaves' work. Despite this racial basis to labouring positions, slaves quickly spilled out into jobs and occupations which the slave traders could never have thought possible. If whites were reluctant to take on slave work, the slaves for their part showed no reluctance in taking on white people's work.

Slaves worked from their early years up to old age or when they ceased to be economically viable. We need to recall that this was true for labouring people the world over; the great bulk of the population in eighteenth-century England were labourers. And they put their offspring to work, especially in the countryside, as soon as they could be usefully employed (watching beasts, scaring birds, helping with the harvest). There was nothing unique about slavery in using the young and the old. What did make slavery distinctive, however, was the discipline of labour, imposed from above, which slaves passed through from their first to their last years.

We have seen that slave-owners sought to keep slaves busy. As soon as a slave child became useful he/she was turned loose on the simplest of tasks (looking after hens, for instance). On Worthy Park estate in Jamaica, children were put to work at the age of 6. That same estate in the 1790s had a 'Fourth Gang' with an average age of 9½. Even the gang above, the 'Third Gang', had an average age of 15½. In the American South, slave children were put into the fields at the age of 10.

Slaves were kept at work until their usefulness ended. In South Carolina, slaves were normally retired at the age of 70, but until then were employed in a series of useful jobs. Visitors often remarked on the antiquity of slaves still at work on slave properties: these 'curious fossil specimens of negro humanity'. Among the slaves, on the other hand, the old ones tended to be respected and revered. Economic uselessness on one side was experience and wisdom on the other. In the Caribbean, slaves were worked to a very great age. Again at Worthy Park, a nurse was employed at the age of 79. Old men were often given the task of watchmen, along with weak slaves (M. Craton, 1978).

What needs to be stressed is that the working lives of the slaves were not static. As they passed from one stage of their lives to another, they moved through different categories of labour. From the simple tasks of childhood through to the simple tasks of old age, slaves were consigned to economically appropriate work. And, like those who were unsaleable from the slave ships, some were rendered useless and uneconomic by illness, accident or age. Slaves were always listed and tabulated in their owners' documents by their level of economic usefulness. Moreover, it is perfectly clear that many slaves found their usefulness seriously – in some cases permanently – undermined by ailments and diseases, some brought from Africa and others related to their immediate environment (R. Sheridan, 1985). We know from detailed studies of West Indian slaves that there were high levels of illness and disability even among the slaves working in the most onerous tasks (J.R. Ward, 1988). Slaves were, then, put to work at tasks thought appropriate to their age and condition, throughout their lives. Life for the slave was an endless cycle of work punctuated by the rhythms of the seasons, social and family life, and by their own efforts to shape a decent life for themselves.

If there was any single group of slaves who seemed more oppressed than most, it was surely the women. Many male slaves moved between different categories, from unskilled to skilled via training in their teens, or into élite and preferential tasks as they showed strength and aptitude. Men even took up jobs thought to be preserved for female slaves (nursing, sewing or cooking, for instance). But women could not be elevated into the élite professions and skills which were vital to the slave economy but which remained exclusively male.

Slave society became a complex social organisation in which work was allocated along a variety of lines: by age, fitness, sex, colour and strength. Nor is it the case that all slaves were treated the same or viewed as an undifferentiated black mass by their employers. Slave-owners valued certain slaves more than others. At its crudest, of course, the slave system could not work without all the skills and labours of the slaves. But within the slave hierarchy, certain kinds of work were more valued than others. We can test this simply by the rewards and benefits given to some slaves and not to others. Elite slaves – the drivers, head men, skilled slaves and the like – received better and more of the basic essentials of life. They were, at times, given small pleasures and luxuries. But the most potent threat held over the heads, and keeping them up to the mark, was the threat of demotion. No skilled slave, a domestic for instance, would ever relish going back to work in the fields.

One of the most interesting groups of slaves was the domestics. It was a sign of a planter's wealth and status that he could afford to surround himself with bevies of retainers for each and every task in and around the house. Clearly the skills required of domestics were not those needed in field hands. The ability to wait on table or to cook were quite different from the brute strength required in cane cutting. It was a sign of the importance slave-owners attached to material consumption and an extravagant display of their wealth that domestics fairly buzzed around them. West Indian planters became the objects of ridicule for their ostentatious use of servants. For the slaves working in the Great House there were obvious advantages. They were shielded from the privations and harships of work in the fields and they had access to a more comfortable life than their peers elsewhere on the plantation. But there were disadvantages. Female slaves were exposed to the sexual advances of white men – advances they were in no position to resist. They were also under the close scrutiny of their masters and, especially, of their mistresses. It was often thought that a cruel or oppressive white mistress could be the most difficult owner of all. And while the domestics were there to make their owners' lives more comfortable, there remained the fear, especially in the West Indies, that the slaves might endanger their owners' lives. The threat of injury or death at the hand of a vengeful domestic was a major element in the planters' demonology.

Whether domestic or field hand, the slave had to be kept at work. They did, as we shall see, have their allowance of free time, and festivals. But their purpose in life was to work. And one purpose of the work they did, quite apart from enriching their owners (and many others) was to keep them in their place. Work was the main instrument for governing the slaves. To control them, to keep them in order, required much more than the whip or the threat of physical punishment. Indeed, in the Caribbean, the slaves greatly outnumbered the whites; brute strength alone could not in itself have guaranteed continuing white control. How to work the slaves, how to keep them in their place, was at the heart of the agricultural problem in the slave colonies.

Slaves' lives were perhaps most miserable when they worked in frontier societies, in conditions of rough privation. But they were also hard-pressed when the local crops were booming and when masters, in the rush to benefit from the market, expanded their lands and slave holdings and pushed their slaves to ever greater efforts.

Slaves and slavery

So pervasive had slavery become that slaves were, by 1800, to be found in an amazing variety of jobs and ranks. In London, there were black musicians, entertainers and boxers. Black sailors were to be seen in ports on both sides of the Atlantic. And in the colonies themselves, slaves could be found working at almost every conceivable task, from the quayside where the ships berthed, to the remotest of rural estates where they toiled in large gangs, producing luxuries for European tables. From the moment the slaves arrived from Africa, or were born into a slave community, their lives thereafter were shaped and dominated by work: work dictated by others, for the betterment of others, in return for which the slaves secured so little. Despite this oppressive régime, slaves were able to secure a better life for themselves than we might at first expect.

6

Slaves at rest

The slave systems throughout America were designed to get the maximum effort from the slaves. But slaves could not work all hours of the day and night. And, in time, it came to be recognised that it made good economic sense to give them a degree of recreation. But the slaves also created leisure for themselves in ways no-one could have predicted.

The social lives of slaves was shaped from their African cultural background but transformed by contact with white society in the Americas; the physical environment in which slaves lived and worked also helped to shape that social live. Much also depended on the ratio of Africans to creoles (local-born); the age and sex ratio of the slaves (it differed if there were more men than women), and the nature of local white society.

Whatever elements of African cultures the slaves imported, they inevitably rubbed up against the dominant local white culture. This was at its most obvious with language. Slaves had to learn a new language (English, Spanish, Portuguese, French or Danish). In the process new languages emerged – patois, pidgin English, for instance – which owed something to both sides.

Slaves so greatly outnumbered the whites in the West Indies that it was inevitable that they would exercise a degree of independence in their lives. On an estate of 500 slaves and ten whites there were obvious limits to white control and scrutiny. It was this African independence which whites throughout the colonies greatly feared. Time and again slave owners sought to purge their slaves of their African roots. But as long as the slave trade continued to bring in fresh imports, the influence would survive. The first thing owners did was to rename the slaves, often changing African names for European, classical or even absurd names. Similarly, slave-owners tried their best to outlaw and present all traces of African 'superstitions'.

Slave religions seemed especially worrying. While slave traders often justified the enslavement of Africans in terms of their 'heathenism', slave-owners in the New World were often reluctant to Christianise their slaves. In the West Indies, Christian churches were weak until the early nineteenth century and the Anglican church had been a local upholder of slavery. Not until the rise of nonconformity and the work of its missionaries in the late eighteenth century was a major effort made to convert local slaves. Thereafter, black Christianity became a potent force in social life throughout the region.

Africans, of course, brought their own beliefs from Africa, with their own ceremonies, rites and priests. But they varied, depending on local tribal customs. In the West Indies they tended to melt into more general slave religions. Ancestor worship and the belief in Obeah (a form of witchcraft) was widespread. With it went local 'priests', prominent local men who exercised great influence over the slaves. They were, from the first, deeply distrusted by whites in general because of their influence over slaves – an influence which did not derive from or depend on the whites themselves. Although the whites feared slave religions, there was little they could do to control them, despite severe penalties and threats. In fact, much of the black priests' work was medical and pastoral. To outsiders,

Medicine

however, it seemed but further evidence of African superstitions. There were variants of these religions, and of white
responses to them, throughout the slave societies of the
Caribbean and South America; yet such beliefs and practices
were rarely accorded the status of a real religion in the
eyes of the local whites. They were simply denounced as
dangerous and barbaric relics of primitive people from a
heathen continent.

From the 1780s in the British colonies, Christianity
made great strides among the slaves. That, too, was disliked
and obstructed by planters. Once again, black religion was
viewed as a vehicle for slave organisation, independent of
the slave-owners. Black chapels and churches fostered the
rise of black preaching and independent black social life.
Black Christians – with the help and encouragement of
their white co-religionists in Britain – began to ask for
freedom, and not just of worship. In sum, black nonconformity gave slaves a vehicle for self-help which was to have
a profoundly corrosive effect on slavery itself (M. Turner,
1985).

In the last fifty years of its existence in the British
Caribbean, black slavery was rapidly becoming Christian.
And after the slave trade was abolished in 1807, the slaves
were increasingly local-born and less and less African in
composition. It was more than mere symbolism that when
the slaves were finally freed throughout the region in 1834,
they showed their thanks by flocking to the nearest church
or chapel.

North American slaves became Christian long before
their cousins in the Caribbean. In North America the slaves
rarely outnumbered local whites. American slaves bred
more easily and the region quickly lost its dependence on
the African slave trade. When American slavery boomed,
following the cotton revolution of the early nineteenth

[67]

century, the cotton states turned, not to Africa for their labour force, but to the fertile slave communities of the old slave states. Thus, American slaves were, from an early date, American: local-born, with local language and cultural patterns. This was also true of their religions; black Christianity was more pronounced and more influential at an earlier date in the United States than it was in the West Indies.

Slaves found the music of Christian worship attractive. Time and again observers noted the 'musicality' of the slaves. Singing in the fields, at home, and in the chapels was obviously a potent form of black self-expression and became an important feature in the make-up of American society. Music was used to help at work, to mock the whites, to amuse and to cheer: to make life and work more tolerable.

Did Christianity itself offer an escape from the brutalities and difficulties of slavery? Churches, chapels and camp meetings offered slaves a place to meet away from their place of work; services were a venue for meeting friends and relatives. And the message they heard from black preachers generally offered a stark contrast to the words they heard from their owners and drivers. At worship, the slaves were a flock, with their own shepherd. He often told of a better world, far removed from earthly miseries.

Slave religions in the Americas were strikingly musical. Observers remarked on what they took to be the African's 'natural' musicality. A Jamaican wrote in 1797: 'Music is a favourite diversion of the Negroes; for the enjoyment of which they are well adopted by a natural good ear.' (*Characteristic Traits*, 1797, 16.) Slave festivals and private celebrations were invariably enjoyed to the vigorous accompaniment of musical instruments and incessant singing and drumming. Slave social life was cause and occasion for music-making on a massive scale, to the pleasure of the slaves and the complaints of local whites. Generally, slaves' musical instruments were improvised from wood, gourds, string, bones, horn and seashells. Parties, balls, holidays and work breaks provided the chance to make music. In 1801 Lady Nugent wrote of Christmas in Jamaica, 'The whole day, nothing but singing, dancing, and noise.' Three years later, the story was much the same: 'Nothing but bonjoes, drums and tom-toms, going all night, and dancing and singing and madness, all the morning. New Year was, if anything even noisier.' (Lady Nugent, 219.)

High days and holidays, mainly Christian festivals or local harvest celebrations, were marked by good food and lavish drink, newly-made clothes and the exchange of gifts. And it was then, especially at Christmas, New Year and the end of the crop, that slave families gathered together, often travelling long distances to meet absent fellow-slaves. Often, too, the world was turned upside down; slaves treated their owners with familiarity and danced and played with them. Planters pandered to their slaves' whims. When Monk Lewis arrived at his Jamaican estate in 1816, his slaves were given the day off. They dressed up, drank plenty of rum, sang and danced for him: 'The singing began about six-o'clock, and lasted without a moment's pause till two in the morning; and never such noise did I hear till then.' (Quoted in Craton *et al.*, 1976, 125.) Such pleasures were carefully devised and encouraged by slave-owners. The end of the festivities was instantly followed by a strict re-imposition of the labouring and racial régime in which all knew their place throughout the labouring day and year. The noise and the colour of the festive celebrations were instantly transmuted into the rigours and privations of the daily slave routines. A world turned upside down for pleasure was put back in its place for work.

It would be wrong, however, to imagine that the slaves were utterly controlled by their owners. Slaves had a certain flexibility over key areas of their lives. Many were allowed to travel and to visit relatives (often sanctioned by 'passes'). Many slaves had a degree of economic independence, growing their own food, keeping animals, and therefore able to exchange foodstuffs for other goods and money in local markets. Of course, much depended on where the slave lived and how buoyant or otherwise was the local industry. When times were hard for their masters, slaves obviously suffered. Yet there were large numbers of slaves who created a much fuller life for themselves than we might initially think possible. The slaves' gardens enriched their lives in many ways; they created, in the West Indies, a system of markets throughout the islands which survive to this day. In the American South, slaves were fond of keeping live-stock, products from which, thought one South Carolina slave owner, 'add materially to their comfort and indul-gences' (C. Joyner, 1984, 129). It was these habits of self-reliance which stood the slaves in such good stead when they were emancipated and obliged thereafter to survive as free black labourers.

These home-grown foods supplemented the meagre supplies provided by the planters. This was especially important in the West Indies. There, in the drive to turn as much land as possible into export production, local food-growing tended to be neglected. Slaves' food was imported from England, Ireland and North America. But in wartime (and the eighteenth century was punctuated by warfare), food supplies were interrupted, so slave-grown foods became extremely important.

Many slaves were able to acquire spare money and a number of material artefacts. At festivals the slaves were famous for the amount of time and effort they invested in dressing up. At celebrations and at weekends, the slaves abandoned their basic work clothes – given by their owners – for more respectable attire. When slaves began to attend church and chapel in the early nineteenth century, they took great pride in appearing clean and smartly dressed. At church the slaves appeared in public among their equals, not as the possessions of someone else, not in the drab clothing given to them as beasts of burden, but as independent people dressed as they saw fit. Not unlike their plebeian counterparts in Britain, the slaves set great store by their 'Sunday best'. But it soon came to an end. As on festival days when the world was turned upside down, this Sunday finery was set aside at the end of the day, and life resumed its routines of toil and punishment.

Slaves in the Americas had a cycle of collective pleasures which we need to set alongside the more brutal existence of their working lives. The family cycles of birth, marriage and death were all enjoyed with appropriate celebrations (few more important than funerals and burials). And in all of these there was a blurred line between the customs of the African homelands and the new, European-influenced customs of the Americas. Music figured prominently at slave funerals, and funerals were commonplace because of the extremely high levels of mortality among the slaves (especially among the young). Slave-owners tended to dislike slave funerals for much the same reason they disliked slave music or social life in general. Here were occasions for slaves to gather independently, to organise among themselves, to discuss and plan. They were moments for autonomous pleasures which normally took place beyond the ken and control of the slave-owners themselves. Whites in slave societies liked to be able to keep their eye on slaves, or at least to know what they were getting up to.

Slave funerals were usually marked by eating and

drinking. Like many peoples in a host of societies, the slaves marked their collective celebrations with foodstuffs. And like other impoverished or deprived people, slaves' feastings were in marked contrast to the meagre daily meals administered by their owners (though supplemented as we have seen by their own foods).

Many aspects of the slaves' social lives showed obvious traces of their African heritage (understandably so among those who were indeed Africans). The way slaves prepared their foods and the utensils they used for cooking were often African. Even the way they spoke, the stories they told and the oral culture they developed were suffused with African elements. Folk songs, stories, tales of the supernatural – all these and more drew upon the varied African experiences of slaves living in the Americas. This African heritage, often difficult to trace now, survived long after the supply of new African imports had been abolished in 1807.

It would be wrong to suggest that the social lives of slaves reveals unalloyed African cultural survivals. As in almost every aspect of the slaves' lives, they had to reconstruct their world anew, using those aspects of their African past which were important or useful but adapting them, now they were in contact with Europeans, to create quite new identities in the Americas. This was noticeable, for instance, with language, with their names and, especially, with the structure of slave family life. Slave families were reconstituted in the colonies. The majority of them, in time, were nuclear families, and those slaves who did not belong to them tended to be imported Africans whose lives had been totally disrupted by the slave trade. It was one of the most remarkable achievements of slave society that stable family life came into being in the slave communities, despite powerful pressures to the contrary. The slave family was the crucible from which many facets of slave life emerged. It was from within the slave family that new generations of slaves learned their rules for life and their values. The practical lessons (child rearing, cooking, health care), moral lessons and religion – these and most other things were learned within the family group. Slaves learned from their families, not from their owners.

It is clearly impossible to describe in any detail the full social lives of slaves, embracing as it does all their non-working hours (and even, in places, aspects of their working lives). But enough has been said to suggest that slaves were able to fashion for themselves a remarkably varied social life. We tend to think of slavery as a total institution which entrapped its victims in an oppressive régime which denied them access to all but life's basic essentials. For many slaves this was certainly the case. There were countless Africans whose lives went unmarked by any saving graces, whose miseries and toils were unrewarded by even the slightest glimmer of enjoyment. And even among those slaves who were able to enjoy the full social life hinted at here, there were obviously many whose daily sufferings could not readily be offset by the occasional pleasure.

It is nontheless important to place the variety of slaves' social experiences alongside the bleaker (and real) image we might have of slavery as a brutal and repressive social system. Even within this system, regarded by many as unflinchingly severe on its victims, room could be created and exploited to make life more tolerable. It may be felt that such pleasures were mere titbits – paltry crumbs which were allowed to fall from the slave owner's table. But for the slaves they were real enough. And it speaks of the slaves' resilience and strength that, despite all that life had imposed on them – enslavement, the Atlantic crossing, adjustment to colonial enslaved life – they found the reserves of strength and adaptability to shape a purposeful social life for themselves and their offspring.

7

Resistance

We have seen at a number of points so far that slave-owners disliked many aspects of the lives of their slaves. They disliked their 'heathenism', thought of them as savages from an uncivilised world, disliked their colour, and generally distrusted everything the slaves did without their own approval or scrutiny. This is part of the slave – slave-owner relationship: a reflection of the distrust and even hatred which the domineering class inevitably exhibits towards its human possessions. But for slave-owners in the Americas, the hatred they developed for their slaves was consolidated by the threats which the slaves posed to the lives and to the well-being of the slave-owners. Slaves did not all passively accept their slavery. Many (not all, but enough to make it a recurring pattern) resisted their condition. Their resistance took a great variety of forms. Historians of a previous generation devoted a great deal of effort to teasing out the nature of slave resistance. We are now in a better position to judge the significance of slave resistance in the broader sweep of slave history in the Americas.

Resistance to slavery began the moment that Africans were first captured and enslaved. We have no way of measuring its extent, but once Africans had been sold to white slave traders we have strong evidence of the levels of resistance. Slaves tried, whenever the opportunity arose, to run away, or on the slave ships to fling themselves overboard and perish. They tried to overwhelm the crew or to hurt them in some way. Vigilance was the major rule for everyone employed on a slaver. Violence and self-destruction seemed to many slaves the only response open to them; the alternative was submission and accommodation. This interplay – resistance and accommodation – was to characterise slave societies throughout their existence.

Once in the New World, the ability of slaves to resist was severely restricted by physical circumstances. On the small West Indian islands, some of them very small indeed, there was nowhere to run to, nowhere to hide. On the bigger islands there was an abundance of bush and mountainous jungle to retreat to, but that posed problems of a different order. Only exceptional people could survive alone in what was often an extremely hostile physical environment; they needed to be able to house, feed and clothe themselves while avoiding detection by the whites.

From the earliest days of Spanish settlement and of the introduction of slaves, blacks ran away. By the time the English took Jamaica in 1655, for example, there were bands of 'Maroons' operating in the island's interior: ex- and runaway slaves living as independent communities. Throughout the history of slavery in the West Indies and South America, such communities were commonplace: maroon gangs and communities, outside the pale of slave society, often threatening it, sometimes at peace with it and sometimes a refuge for fresh runaways. There are a number of communities which survive to this day whose origins lay in these early runaways from slave society (R. Price, 1978; G. Heuman, 1986). Slaves ran away even before they got to their new homes. On the trek from the quayside to their first place of employment, slaves ran off into the bush if the opportunity arose. Runaways were so common in colonial Virginia that the Assembly passed laws in 1705 and 1722 specifying how Africans, unable to speak English and unable to name their masters, were to be recaptured. In Maryland some Africans ran away and joined local Indians; others simply perished. It was widely accepted among slave-owners that Africans would habitually run away before they had been settled into their new régimes. Maryland decided that, after a year, such runaways should have an ear cut off and have 'R' branded on their chin. There were a number of small runaway communities on the frontiers in Virginia and Maryland (A. Kulikoff, 1986, 328–9).

The evidence for slaves running away becomes volum-inous as the colonies were maturing and had their own legal and literary traditions. Wills, estate papers, but above all else newspaper advertisements returned time and again to runaway slaves, asking for their return, offering rewards and listing slaves as missing. There was a veritable army of slaves regularly slipping away from its owners. Often they were recaptured (sometimes after a considerable period of freedom), often they returned voluntarily, sometimes they disappeared permanently, lost to the bush – to the Indians, to the animals – which lay just beyond the pale of settled society in the Northern Colonies. Running away was so frequent that one South Carolina planter simply advertised 'that many of the slaves belonging to the plantation of JOHN WALTERS Esq are constantly running away' (G. Heuman, 1986, 58).

One researcher has counted 3,558 runaways listed in South Carolina colonial newspapers. Many of those slaves were valuable, skilled, acculturated and therefore unlike the freshly-imported Africans. In addition there were 2,041 advertisements for captive slaves, the majority of whom were Africans and recent arrivals. Overall it seems that Africans, rather than creole (local-born) slaves were the typical permanent runaways. This is as we might expect;

those born into slavery, more acculturated to its demands and prospects (such as they were), and with no personal experience of an alternative world, were less likely to escape. Of course, the Africans were described as unskilled; skilled runaways were more valuable and it was more important to recover them.

As more slaves acquired skills, and were able to establish a modest position for themselves and their kinfolk within the slave system, powerful incentives emerged which secured slaves to their places of work. More often than not, runaways in the North American colonies were heading for a specific place: to see friends, loved-ones and relatives. This was strikingly true among women runaways, the very great majority of whom were intent on visiting. And those runaways who were skilled and could speak English might try to pass themselves off as free blacks. But the over-whelming majority of runaways, certainly in colonial South Carolina and the Chesapeake, intended simply to visit slaves on other plantations. They were not so much resisting slavery as such, but rather trying to shape a fuller social world for themselves in a society which sought to limit their freedom.

The evidence from runaway advertisements is very revealing. In South Carolina, slaves went to great lengths to visit friends and relatives, or to return to places they liked and where they preferred to live. Often they travelled with a friend or relative. And the great majority of the runaways were young men. What these details show is the importance of slave kinship and community ties.

In the West Indies the pattern was similar, but with major differences. Much depended on geography. On Barbados (the size of the Isle of Wight), once the land was fully used, where could slaves run to without being caught? In the early days slaves (and indentured servants) did escape to the

woods. But even then, many of the runaways were trying
to make contacts on other properties. Others simply took
to the sea, leaving the island in whatever vessel came to
hand, to smaller islands not yet fully conquered, or to join
ships that might take them. Warfare was so common that
there were often warships of other nations willing to take
slaves on board as crew members.

Despite the absence of obvious physical escape routes
in so populated an island, runaways were common on
Barbados up to the end of slavery. There, as in South
Carolina, the majority of runaways were young males.
Many of the Barbadian runaways tried to pass themselves
off as free people: easier to do, perhaps, for those (a substantial number) who were skilled or semi-skilled workers.

Most runaways in Barbados quit their plantations in mid-
summer (when the crops had been harvested), at the time
when their owners might have been at their most lax and
when food was notoriously short. The great majority of such
runaways stayed away only for a short period, returning
voluntarily or being recaptured.

In the West Indies as in North America, such data confirms the strength the slaves attached to their family and
community ties; large numbers of them ran the risk of
severe punishments in order to visit friends and loved-ones.
Wherever research has been conducted on runaways –
maronage, to use the technical term – the findings have
local variations throughout the slave colonies. But it
confirms the broad outlines of slave runaways described
here.

In addition to individual runaways there were, as we have
seen, ex-slave communities (Maroon communities) lurking
on the edges of many slave societies. Those in North
America were small and short-lived. As the frontier expanded westward they were absorbed or destroyed, like the

communities of native peoples. But in the bigger islands and in South America a number of them thrived. They were to be found, for instance, in Colombia, in Surinam and in Jamaica.

The Jamaican maroons proved a major problem to slave-owning society. They raided plantations for food, goods and women; they harassed slave-owners, gave a home to run-aways (though this was eventually stopped) and were in general a continuing worry to the slave society around them. Eventually, the British authorities conceded Maroon independence in a peace treaty in 1795–6. It was a sign of the strength and resilience of the Maroons that they forced the military and colonial authorities to treat with them. The maroons were difficult to beat in the field – or rather, in the bush (where they often proved the guerrilla superior to British troops and local militia) – so instead the British were forced reluctantly to treat with them. It was a remark-able turn of events: a slave-owning power negotiating with ex-slaves and accepting their freedom.

Slaves sought to resist or modify their bondage in a host of ways. While it is tempting to imagine that flight or violent resistance was the natural, obvious form of resist-ance, there were many other, less striking but at times more effective (and less dangerous) ways of resisting. In fact, the story of slave resistance ranges from outright bloody revolt through to a host of almost undetectable tricks designed to hurt their owners' interests. Foodstuffs were stolen, gardens raided. Slaves lied to their masters. In all slave societies, slave-owners regularly complained that they could never rely on their slaves; they lied, they were duplicitous and untrustworthy. We need to remember that, in part, this attitude towards the slave was part of a broadly-based caricature of slaves which emerged throughout the course of slavery and which served to justify slavery itself. Like black indolence and stupidity, the slave's habit of lying was used by slave-owners to justify how the slaves were treated. Lying was a slave response; why always tell the truth when it might at times merely bring wrath and punishment? Slavery, said one American ex-slave, 'makes its victims lying and mean; for which vices it afterwards reproaches them, and uses them as arguments to prove that they deserve no better fate' (E.D. Genovese, 1975, 609). Slaves lied, they stole, they dragged their feet and worked as slowly and sometimes as unproductively as possible. The lash and the beatings did not always succeed. Slave-owners tried to build incentives into their work systems, but they too were rarely as effective as desired. Slaves also damaged their place of work. They damaged crops and animals; stole, ate or sold the crops they harvested; hobbled animals, and sometimes struck their owners directly. Slaves set fire to the fields, to their owners' property. Attacks on whites were common throughout slave societies; they also incurred the most savage of penalties. It is understandable why slaves struck or hurt their masters and mistresses. There was a limit to the amount of punishment, insults or physical assault a person could take. Despite knowing what would happen to them, slaves reared up in anger, struck their owners, sometimes killed them – in a premeditated fashion or spontaneously – and then had to flee or simply await the inevitable retribution.

Slaves were often accused of poisoning their owners. Often the accusations were false (so many people died suddenly and unexpectedly in the pre-modern world, especially in the tropics), and the finger of suspicion was invariable pointed at local (often domestic) slaves. We know of a number of poisonings and attempted poisonings – sometimes mass poisonings. But we also know of many less convincing cases where innocent slaves were accused of plotting the death or illness of their stricken owners.

Such acts of violence – real or imaginary – brought a fearful punishment. Violence was, as we have seen, basic to slavery and the slave system. But even by contemporary standards, the punishments meted out to the slaves were horrifying. In 1675 slaves involved in a plot in Barbados were sentenced to be burned alive, some to be beheaded and others dragged through the streets. A rebel in Antigua in 1687 was 'burned to ashes'; another had his leg and his tongue cut off 'as a Living Example to the rest' (Walvin, 1983, 107). By the early nineteenth century, when cruelties of all kinds were increasingly disliked in Britain, slaves continued to suffer barbaric penalties which, perhaps acceptable to the seventeenth century, caused offence 200 years later. Slave-owners tried to keep in place a barbaric and draconian code of punishment which caused increased offence to more civilised opinion. By the early nineteenth century it seemed to many in Britain that the true savagery in the slave colonies was to be found among the planters, not among the slaves.

The most worrying of all plantocratic nightmares (of which there were large numbers) was open revolt. Individual violence, however endemic, could normally be contained. Much more threatening, however, was revolt. The fear of revolt figured prominently in the literature of slave societies, from their first days to their demise. Indeed, even before the slaves landed in America, the slave traders were, as we have seen, ever alert to the possibility of revolt. In the colonies, planters saw signs of revolt on all sides. In many cases, they were justified in their worries. As often as not, their imagination ran wild. Plots, rumours of plots, whispers of revolt, garbled messages from slaves and other slave-owners: these formed the stuff of slave-owners' conversations and alarms. The simple truth was that they could not relax, could not afford to ignore the most innocent of slave gestures and threats. Revolt was a common response of the slaves throughout the New World.

Open revolt was much more common in some slave societies than others. In North America it was much less common and much less violent than it was in the West Indies. In the Chesapeake area, revolts were unusual (though rumours of revolt were much more common) (A. Kulikoff, 1986, 329–30). In Jamaica, the history of the island, until freedom in 1838 could almost be written in terms of slave revolt and resistance. Major uprisings in North America were more unusual. Among the most notable were the Stono revolt in South Carolina in 1739, Gabriel Prosser's revolt in Virginia in 1800, the panic among whites in Louisiana in 1811, Denmark Vesey's plot of 1822, and Nat Turner's revolt in Virginia in 1831. Although these are celebrated events in the history of North American slavery, compared to the convulsions in the Caribbean (and Brazil) they were tiny.

The Nat Turner revolt mustered perhaps seventy slaves. In Jamaica it has been argued that the average numbers of slaves involved in the island's regular revolts was upwards of 400. By the mid-eighteenth century scarcely a decade had passed without a major revolt. In 1760, 1,000 slaves were involved. In the seventeenth and eighteenth centuries, the Jamaican slave revolts were really African revolts. There was often a contagion of revolt, with rumour fanning rumour and violence begetting violence, and a ghastly pattern became familiar; black violence was quelled and then punished by white retribution on an even more horrifying scale (M. Craton, 1983, 198).

It is hard to provide a series of causes for such revolts, but there seem to be certain obvious and important factors. The ratio between black and white was crucial; blacks greatly outnumbered whites in the West Indies, but this was rarely so in North America. Slave-owners made great efforts – generally unsuccessful – to maintain a reasonable balance between black and white. The ratio of African to creole was also important. Many slave societies were in effect African societies and the sheer concentration of imported Africans could often prove disastrous. This was less of a problem in North America where the slaves rapidly began to breed and to keep up their numbers. The West Indies, on the other hand, always needed fresh supplies from Africa.

The most savage and successful of slave revolts was that in San Domingue (Haiti) in the 1790s, when, inspired initially by the French Revolution, the largely African population of that French colony overthrew the slave system. But it was a unique event which, though sending its ripples through all other West Indian slave societies, had no counterpart elsewhere (D. Geggus, 1981; R. Blackburn, 1988).

Perhaps the most unusual aspect of the major slave revolts in the British islands was that the worst incidents erupted in the last years of slavery: not when slavery was at its worst, but in the years when the abolitionist campaigns in Britain were apparently making headway towards securing black freedom. There were three revolts – Barbados (1816), Demerara (1823) and Jamaica (1831) which shook the British slave system to its core.

These were the most important of all revolts in the British slave colonies. They came after the slave trade had been abolished (in 1807) and at a time when the campaign for full emancipation was building up in Britain. There were, of course, particular causes for revolt in each case, but the underlying trends were clear enough. The islands' slave populations were becoming ever more creole (i.e., with an ever smaller proportion of Africans). Planters had to make do with their existing slave stock, and in order to make up the shortfall they began to readjust their slave labour force, so that slaves who might have expected better jobs found themselves working in the fields. There was a consequent frustration among the slaves.

Perhaps most important of all, the slaves were increasingly Christian. The missionaries had effectively penetrated the slave quarters, and powerful black preachers began to emerge from local chapels. These men became the spokesmen for their communities, and on much broader issues than simple religion. The language and imagery of the Bible – especially of the Old Testament – was readily converted to the slaves' conditions. Images of a better life to come, the language of equality, the promise of salvation, the custom of preaching among the slaves: all these and more served to radicalise the slaves as never before. Throughout the islands, leaders of these revolts were prominent in their local chapels. It is clear why the planters had resisted the coming of the missionaries.

On top of this was the shadow of the abolitionist movement in Britain: the mounting campaign in public and Parliament to free the slaves. Word about the progress of that campaign was quickly fed into the slave quarters. Planters talked carelessly about it at their tables, and their domestics simply relayed the word – often garbled – back to their friends. The island newspapers were full of it.

The slaves were in no doubt that the British people were actively discussing their freedom. Indeed, rumours abounded that freedom had already been conceded but was being withheld by the slave-owners. All of this made for a volatile mix. And each island had its own distinctive problem to add to the overall brew. The slave revolts of 1816, 1823 and 1831 followed a well-trodden path. Initial

black violence against persons and property was followed
by savage reprisals. The mass butchery of slaves (many of
whom were, to repeat, Christians) caused great offence in
Britain. The British were developing a new sensibility
about certain kinds of violence. Perhaps more importantly,
they were deeply offended by the new of the persecution
of fellow Christians. There was a growing community of
nonconformists in Britain. Missionaries returning from
the islands told them of the sufferings of their black co-
religionists. There emerged a sense of despair about the
slave colonies; if they could only be maintained at such
cost, were they really worth keeping? How could Britain
justify slavery if it was a system kept in place only by dint
of regular acts of outrageous violence against the slaves? Of
course, one answer was that slavery made great profits for
Britain, but even that seemed less convincing by the early
nineteenth century.

Open slave revolt was only the most memorable and
dramatic form of slave resistance. Slaves came to terms
with their enslavement and life of bondage in a host of ways.
It would be wrong to suggest that all slaves resisted. It is,
of course, impossible to assess the numbers, the pro-
portions, of slaves who positively fought the system as best
they could: by running away, by refusing to work hard or
properly, by acts of violence or plots. It seems much more
likely that the great majority came to terms with their
condition – not happily, but nonetheless accommodating
themselves grudgingly to a system they found hard to alter.
Slavery was a system which, in any case (and as we have
seen) allowed slaves to fashion important aspects of their
lives for themselves, without the intrusive scrutiny of their
owners. Slaves were in certain respects in charge of their
own lives and created for themselves, their kinsfolk and
community some semblance of a full life.

Many slaves went through different phases, at one time resisting, at another coming to terms with their lot. A young, newly-arrived African might bridle and rear up. That same man, older, hardened to the harsh ways of the planters, might rein in his anger and feelings and resist the natural temptation to fight the system, the owners or their agents.

Yet it is clearly wrong to think of slaves' responses in terms of stark alternatives: to resist or to accommodate. There were myriad ways of living the life of a slave. It is undoubtedly true that slave resistance was a characteristic of black slavery throughout its history. The story of that resistance, in all its diverse forms, has been one of the most revealing discoveries of historians of the past generation. But is also leaves much untold. For every slave who struck back, who resisted his or her lot in some particular way, how many others simply turned the other cheek?

8

Ending slavery

Black slavery in the British colonial empire had evolved
slowly over a long period as a response to changing economic needs, buttressed by local and metropolitan law and
finally secured by racial discrimination. Its ending came
comparatively quickly and, in some respects, unexpectedly.
Few people criticised the slave system before the mid-1780s
either on moral or economic grounds. From 1787 onwards,
however, its critics thrived, growing in numbers, stridency
and political influence. It was to take fifty years for the slave
system to be destroyed (the slave trade was abolished in
1807 and slaves were finally freed in 1838 – both cases by
Acts of Parliament).

Not surprisingly, historians have argued more fiercely
about the ending of slavery than about any other aspect of
its history. The crucial area of debate has been the connection – if any – between the fact of the British turning
against slavery and the fact that this was at a time when
Britain was being transformed by the initial impact of
industrial capitalism. For many years the campaigns against
the slave trade, and then against slavery, were portrayed as
a triumph for the rising tide of outraged Christian feeling;
the British people, fired by new-found Christian zeal,
decided to end the moral outrage that was black slavery. In
this interpretation, one man – William Wilberforce –
stood out as the prime mover. He was God's Englishman
who persuaded the nation and Parliament to renounce its

wicked ways. In fact, Wilberforce's role has been greatly misunderstood, in large part because earlier historians relied too heavily on the propaganda created by his sons after his death.

This account (though in fact there were many variants on it) which looks to Wilberforce and the spread of evangelical spirit as the prime cause of abolition, has been rejected by most historians since the Second World War. But historians of abolition seem to agree only on their rejection of the old orthodoxy. No single alternative explanation of abolition has secured the unqualified loyalty of all historians, most of whom continue to dispute the course and nature of the ending of the British slave system (see the bibliographical guide at the end of this volume).

At first glance it might seem odd that historians have argued so fiercely about the ending of British slavery. Closer inspection quickly reveals why. Black slavery, for so long a source of material well-being to the Mother Country, lay at the heart of a remarkably complex commercial, strategic and political system. It drew together, as we have seen, Britain, Africa and the Americas – to say nothing of the broader commercial links with Asia. Why should Britain turn against and then destroy so vast a system which had served its purpose so well for a century and a half? Was the ending of slavery, like its inception, an economic phenomenon?

Black slavery in the Americas was economic rather than racial in its origins and growth. Although that may now seem obvious, cases have been made that black slavery was made inevitable by the physical suitability of Africans for labour in the tropics. Once the pioneering settlements had given way to large-scale cultivation of tropical staples – sugar, tobacco and rice – African labour provided the ideal solution. Economies of scale determined the use of the one form of labour which seemed to be readily available in vast and apparently limitless supply; the Europeans turned to Africa.

The use of African labour had little to do with racial thinking in the first instance. Africans had long been objects of curiosity in Europe, and Europeans had a series of distinctive attitudes towards black humanity which some historians have regarded as the origins of modern racism. But to be black did not necessarily mean to be cast in the role of permanent slave. Yet by the time slavery had matured in Jamaica, Virginia, and later in the Southern United States, to be black had come to mean being a slave.

We can measure this by the difficulty free blacks experienced in proving their freedom. It was an indication of the ubiquity of black slavery and of the automatic connection between blackness and slavery, that all blacks in the mature colonies were assumed to be slaves. To be black was to be a slave, and to be a slave was the mark of the greatest economic and social stigma. No self-respecting white person would undertake slave work; such work was fit only for blacks. Thus there developed that complex historical formula of racism, the legacy of which lives on (in transmuted form) to the present day. It may, again, seem ironic that the begetters of so much wealth in Britain (and later America) should inherit as their reward the mark of racial inferiority.

What happened throughout the colonies was the creation, by the plantocratic élites and their metropolitan supporters, of a racist ideology which buttressed their economic and labour interests. Legal and political vocabulary incorporated the view of the slave as a thing, a species of property. But we need to stress the degree to which this represented a revolution in British thinking. When the colonies were first settled there had *not* been an English legal, social or economic tradition of viewing the black as a slave, as a chattel. This view has emerged as a consequence and as an essential by-product of the development of slavery itself. Slavery, in the words of two recent historians of the subject, was 'a cheap supply of labour, with certain productivity and costs, whose adoption was determined by considerations of profit maximization'. Yet the study of slavery and its abolition before World War II had effectively neglected the economic origins of slavery. Not until the publication of *Capitalism and Slavery* by the Trinidadian scholar Eric Williams in 1944 was the centrality of that economic formula established. But ever since, historians have disputed the details of the economic interpretation of slavery and abolition (B. Solow and S.L. Engerman, 1988).

From its earliest days, the link between Europe and the American colonies was embryonic capitalism in operation. Cheap land in the colonies, worked by African slave labour, was financed by European capital to produce great profits through the cultivation of tropical staples. As we have seen, goods and services were generated by the slave system: shipping and banking, the merchant houses of British ports serving the major maritime trade to Africa and the Americas. British goods from a range of industries were devoured by Africa and the colonies. In return the slave colonies spat forth luxury goods demanded by a growing army of European consumers.

There are obvious indicators of the wealth the slave colonies generated for Britain: the splendid homes and retreats of the plantocratic class, the physical growth of the slave ports, and the industrial facilities created to handle the tropical imports (of sugar, rum, tobacco and rice). It was, in the words of an early-eighteenth-century observer, 'a magnificent superstructure of American commerce and naval power on an African foundation' (B. Solow and S. L. Engerman, 1988, 5).

When stated at such a level of generality, few would disagree with the thesis connecting slavery with British economic buoyancy. But the debate becomes much more contentious when focused on the finer details of that economic relationship. Most debatable of all has been the claim (again effectively initiated by Eric Williams) that it was profits from slavery which 'provided one of the main streams of that accumulation of capital in England which financed the Industrial Revolution' (B. Solow and S. L. Engerman, 1988, 5). Although this line of argument has been fiercely attacked, there are other contemporary historians who argue that the slave system was indeed much more instrumental in generating British industrial growth in the late eighteenth century than many now accept. It has been claimed, for instance, that the slave system created an enormous common market for Britain, and that by the eighteenth century Britain was edging towards industrialisation thanks to the Atlantic trade's impact on the growth of trade, transport and manufacture. By that period there was indeed a major upturn in demand for sugar, and a shift towards British industrial production. The slave colonies, by the late eighteenth century, were generating increased purchasing power, and the Atlantic trade may have consumed more than half of British domestic products. Though it is widely accepted that the slave system did not dispatch vast amounts of money to be invested in the early industrial revolution, slavery did generate huge investments in the Empire, profits from which enhanced purchasing power in Britain itself.

The economic ramifications of the slave system went far beyond mere profit to the Mother Country. There was, for instance, a vast quantity of British exports to North

America, where much of the purchasing power grew from the Northern Colonies' involvement in the Atlantic trade. At a time when British manufactured exports to Europe fell markedly, exports to the colonial Empire grew dramatically. And this colonial demand was substantially rooted in the slave labour of the West Indies and the American slave colonies. What the slave system did was to enrich Britain: to make it 'more commercial and more industrial'. (B. Solow and S. L. Engerman, 1988, 10). The exact manner in which this took place has been the concern of two generations of economic historians writing since Eric Williams' volume was published.

Some indication of the importance of slavery to Britain can be gleaned from its demise. If it is true that the slave system was of major material consideration, then it would seem logical to argue that the system was brought to an end when it ceased to be profitable, or perhaps when other more profitable avenues of economic activity were opened up to those involved in the slave system.

It has been a durable plank of Eric Williams' thesis that the British abolished their slave empire because of its declining profitability. Williams was keen to debunk an older school of imperial historians who had argued that slavery had succumbed to the power of British evangelicalism.

The ending of the slave system is still associated in the popular mind with William Wilberforce and his colleagues. And it was part of those evnaglicals' own propaganda to promote the feeling that slavery had crumbled before the onslaught of powerful Christian sentiment in Britain. It is perfectly true that there was a great deal of Christian sentiment directed against the slave trade and slavery in its last phase. And it is also true that nonconformist chapels and organisations were very important in rallying public opinion against the slave system. But if outraged Christianity is thought to have undermined slavery, why did it take so long to achieve it? Where was the Christian voice of complaint in the early or middle years of slavery? In fact, the formal organised Christian voice, in Britain at least, was notably silent throughout much of the history of colonial slavery. The voices of outrage were few and far between and generally went unheeded in the gathering rush to build the slave system and profit from it. But in his determination to reduce the previously unchallenged role of the evangelicals, Eric Williams seriously misunderstood their importance. It is now possible to argue that Christian opinion was indeed important in ending the slave system, but it would have been to no avail had not the determining social and economic context changed dramatically; that changed because of industrial and urban growth.

In the immediate aftermath of Eric Williams' book, it came to be widely accepted that the British ended their involvement with slavery primarily because of the economic decline of the West Indies. That argument (one which has gained widespread acceptance, especially through school books, on both sides of the Atlantic) is as follows (though this must of necessity be a crude approximation). The old slave system had been forged from an attachment to mercantilism and protectionism. But British economic interest in the slave trade and slavery began to wane with the rise of industrial capitalism. What British interests now required was an economy steered by free trade rather than by restriction. Moreover, the British began to lose their commitment to the West Indies at the moment when those slave islands and the slave trade which fed them were in a process of decline.

This economic interpretation (that British abolition was a function of the economic decline of the slave empire) has been under strenuous attack for the past decade. A new group of historians have persuasively argued that far from declining, the British West Indies were actually enjoying boom years at the very time the British decided to end first the slave trade, and later, slavery. The Acts of Parliament which finished the slave system are now seen, by this particular group of historians, as flying in the teeth of British economic self-interest (S. Drescher, 1987).

If this argument is true, it raises some difficult questions about the relationship between political decision-making and economic self-interest in the years between 1787 and 1834. At first glance it seems hard to accept that Parliament could enact legislation which ran so diametrically counter to the nation's material well-being. We need, therefore, to make some observations on the abolition movement itself.

The first group to organise in Britain against the slave system was a nucleus of evangelicals, largely noncon-formists, who campaigned from 1787 to end the slave trade. Their propaganda campaign was superb. A nationwide network of abolitionist organisations was formed, evidence was accumulated from the slave ports, massive petitions were launched, and MPs and Parliament were successfully lobbied about the evils of the slave trade. From the beginning, the West Indian interests were on the defensive and could never match the publicity or popularity of abolition. As nonconformity grew, so too did the abolition campaign, for it had an expanding network of chapels and lecture circuits, especially in the newer urban and industrial communities, to feed into. It is now clear that the slave trade could have been ended earlier than 1807; only accidents of timing and poor parliamentary discipline allowed abolition-ist votes to fail (J. Hayward, 1986).

Ending the slave trade was a remarkable achievement, which was carried through in a relatively short period.

But would it have been possible if the slave system had remained economically vital to Britain? Some historians continue to argue that it was the loss of the American colonies in 1776 which dealt the slave system a mortal blow, for the economic importance of the Northern Colonies to the West Indies was vital. But the more convincing arguments have been advanced by historians whose evidence shows that the slave system remained as viable, as profitable and as expansive as ever: better, indeed, than ever before. One historian has argued that the West Indies remained as important in the years 1828–32 as they had been in the mid-eighteenth century. The arguments revolve around economic details – the levels of profits from particular aspects of the slave empire (the slave trade, the plantations, the exports of British goods) – and it is often difficult to steer a clear path through the minutiae of the arguments. What is generally accepted, however, is that the abolition of the slave trade in 1807 did have major repercussions.

Abolitionists hoped that ending the supply of Africans to the colonies would force planters to treat their slaves better; denied access to new Africans, the planters would make the lives of their existing slaves better from necessity, owing to the need to get them to breed successfully. In the event this did not really happen. It is true that some planters sought to encourage better breeding among their slaves. But they were at the mercy of forces they could not control, namely the age structure and sex ratio of their slaves. In shifting slaves around their properties in order to manage the properties more efficiently, planters created frustrations and resentments among many slaves. It was this mood of resentment which proved so important in the slave revolts of 1816, 1823 and 1831.

There were other factors which were shifting the focus

of Britain's economic interest. As the British population grew in the early nineteenth century, it − not the export markets − began to absorb a growing proportion of British production. British economic growth was being substantially fuelled by domestic consumption. Moreover, in the diminished world of early-nineteenth-century exports, it was India, Australia and Latin America, rather than the countries of the old Empire, which became Britain's best customers (B. Solow and S. L. Engerman, 1988, 14).

What is beyond dispute is the remarkable following which the anti-slavery movement was able to develop by the late 1820s. It was the most successful of the great nineteenth-century pressure groups (like Chartism, Sabbatarianism and others). Its ambitions were fully achieved. In 1807 the British stopped slave trading and thereafter spent a great deal of naval and diplomatic effort preventing other nations from slave trading. By the mid 1820s the campaign was renewed, this time to end slavery itself. It was a fluctuating campaign carried along, after 1830, by the broader and parallel movement to reform Parliament itself. With the passing of the 1832 Reform Act, the ending of slavery was assured. The change of personnel in the Commons ensured a greater body of MPs sympathetic to black freedom. Members from the older constituencies tended to support the continuation of slavery. But those from newer, urban and to a degree industrial communities (where nonconformity was important) were wedded to abolition.

Pressure on Parliament from the abolition movement was intense. There had never been such broadly-based public backing for a reforming movement, from poorer plebeian communities through to the intellectual élite which had, throughout, formed the nucleus of the movement. The abolitionist case was best expressed through waves of petitions which included tens of thousands of names. And MPs were persuaded to support black freedom by pressure from their constituencies. There is no doubt that demands for the end of slavery were genuinely popular throughout the length and breadth of Britain, and the popularity of abolition was a key element in securing the passage of emancipation through Parliament.

When emancipation came, it did so in stages. Parliament conceded freedom via an Apprenticeship scheme from 1834. Ex-slaves were obliged to work for nothing for their ex-owners for a certain number of hours per week; thereafter they were free to pursue their own activities for pay. In some islands, and for some categories of slaves, freedom came completely in 1834. Moreover, the slave-owners were compensated to the tune of £20 million for the loss of their slaves. In effect, the British Parliament had bought the slaves' freedom. Why not, some abolitionists argued, compensate the slaves?

By the time the British freed their slaves in 1838 there were few people in Britain prepared to stand up in public and defend the slave system. Even those who sought to support its economic importance felt obliged to concede its moral crudity. This constituted a major revolution in attitudes. Even the founding abolitionists in 1787 had only sought to end the slave trade. Now, in 1838, the whole British slave system had been brought down.

The initial campaign launched against the slave trade in the 1780s had quickly gained acceptance among the 'enlightened'. In the 1790s it took even firmer root among the early plebeian radicals – the Corresponding Societies – before all forms of radical activity were banned in the fierce reaction against the excesses of (and the ensuing war against) the French Revolution. When the campaign against slavery itself was launched in the late 1820s, it won to its side more and more men (and large numbers of women) from a number of British élites. Most significant of all, perhaps, was the growing support for black freedom among men and women who were committed to the new economic order in Britain: to a capitalist system which deplored economic restraints (on labour, capital or management). The virtues and personal qualities which so many people in Britain found praiseworthy, the qualities which were transforming Britain into a unique economic power, were the antithesis of the slave system. Slavery depended on a highly protective economic system; it denied slaves access to the benefits of wages and denied their owners the obvious benefits of free labour.

By the 1820s in Britain there had developed a powerful cult of anti-slavery. It was part of a more broadly-based sensibility which derived from the late-eighteenth-century enlightenment and had come to unite the propertied and the propertyless in a shared dismissal of the economic and social benefits of slavery. Slavery was seen both as evil and uneconomic: an affront to master and man, an outrage, in the context of a new sense of Christian (primarily nonconformist) zeal. Because slavery was so distant – 5,000 miles away from the homeland – it was easy for diverse groups to unite in their opposition to it. The only people likely to suffer from its demise were the planters. And their violent reactions in the recent slave revolts had shown them to be beyond the pale. Those nearer to home who might suffer from black freedom – the manufacturers, shippers and the like – were faced by an expanding range of alternative markets for their products and energies. It was seen that it might even be more profitable – and certainly less risky – to provide goods, foodstuffs and services to the expanding British population than to the slaves of the West Indies. In the attack on slavery, morality and economic self-interest became cosy bed-fellows.

The campaign for black freedom was greatly helped by a changing climate of opinion, but recent historians have tended to overlook the degree to which that climate was significantly altered by the abolitionists themselves. It was their efforts, within British urban life, and especially from the late 1820s onwards, which won over more and more people to their side. Many of their arguments may well have been suited to the changing needs of the emergent capitalist order, but the abolitionists were first and foremost important as a uniquely successful pressure group, inside and outside Parliament. It was, after all, the abolitionists who, in the last resort, persuaded Parliament to end the British addiction to black slavery.

9

The legacy

The campaigns organised by the abolitionists between 1787 and 1838 had long periods of inactivity: downturns in the abolitionist momentum. In retrospect, however, the campaigns were a remarkably successful and unique political phenomenon. They were crucial in ending both the slave trade and then slavery, both of which were brought to an end by Acts of Parliament. To pass those Acts, Parliament, Ministers (and the Civil Service) had to be persuaded of the importance of abolition. Clearly, pressure from evangelicals was not solely responsible for those Acts, but the recent interest in social history – especially the social history of slave society – has often deflected attention away from the crucial detailed political mechanics of abolition and emancipation. The most difficult task facing current and future historians of the subject is to integrate the two perspectives: to illustrate the precise interplay between social changes in Britain and the slave colonies, and the parliamentary movement towards abolition and emancipation.

The abolitionists' campaign did much more than undermine slavery. They put in place major organisations, and created a momentum for evangelical reform which could not easily be stopped when black slavery was ended in the British Empire in 1838. The Anti-Slavery Society, for instance, survives to this day. There was, furthermore, a continuing need for vigilance on the part of those active in anti-slavery. The British prided themselves in ending their own form of slavery and continued to remind and congratulate themselves on their achievements throughout the nineteenth century. Indeed, the granting of black freedom became an extraordinarily potent element in British self-awareness throughout the century. It was fostered by the continuing abolitionist campaign and by popular literature of all sorts (and was especially influential in children's literature and later in school books). In perpetuating the idea of a uniquely humane people inspired by a unique Christian zeal, all sight was lost of the nation's prior involvement in the story of the slave trade and slavery.

The first and most pressing task facing abolitionists after 1838 was to stop slave trading throughout the world. Despite a flurry of treaties with (largely client) African states, and despite a major Royal Naval presence in the Atlantic and the Indian Oceans, this was largely unsuccessful. More Africans were carried across the Atlantic after 1807 than in the previous century. The reason was straightforward. The economic boom in Brazil and Cuba (for coffee and tobacco) demanded ever-more workers. Enterprising and daring slave traders ran the gauntlet of abolitionist navies knowing, like many before them, that the potential rewards were very great (D. Eltis, 1987).

Slavery survived in the Americas, long after British emancipation. In the United States it survived until the Civil War, in Cuba until 1886, and in Brazil until 1888. The British West Indian sugar economy, on the other hand, had to function without slaves. It declined dramatically for a host of reasons. Many ex-slaves simply left their plantations, but elsewhere they remained (often because of the lack of real alternatives). Planters continued to demand new labour (blaming emancipation for all their problems). The Colonial Office and Parliament obliged with a scheme establishing indentured Indian labour. Boat-loads of Indians were shipped from India to the Caribbean. By the time that scheme was ended, in 1919, Indians had been settled throughout the West Indies (and in other colonial settlements around the world) (H. Tinker, 1974). The British imperial demand for labour had populated vast regions of the Americas with not only Africans and their descendants, but after emancipation, also with Indians and their offspring. There were to be variants on this pattern throughout the new Empire when the labour vacuum created by initial white settlement sucked in armies of poor migrant peoples: Chinese to Canada and the West Indies, Indians to South and East Africa and the South Pacific, and many others scattered across the world.

The British involvement with slavery – along with that of other European nations – had profound and in many respects incalcuable consequences for black Africa itself. Did it lead directly, as Walter Rodney has argued, to the 'underdevelopment' of Africa? Or was the slave trade less catastrophic than that? This is an argument which currently attracts some of the most talented of Africanists in Europe, Africa and North America (W. Rodney, 1981; P. Lovejoy, 1987).

The legacy in the Americas is much more obvious. Today, one-tenth of the population of the United States is descended from slaves. In the British West Indies the proportion is much higher. As we have seen, one major element in the history of slavery was the creation of an ideology of inferiority. Blacks came to be viewed as greatly inferior to whites. The degree to which this was an extension of earlier ideas, and the extent to which it was a direct and conscious creation of the slave system, continues to excite historical debate. Yet it is surely impossible to imagine racial attitudes evolving *as they did* without the slave system which defined and used millions of Africans as things. One major legacy has been the inevitable sense of bitterness and alienation which has influenced many black communities in the Americas and, more recently, in Britain. Much of that bitterness has been directed against modern forms of racism which, though rooted in the slave experience, have been transmuted over the last century by quite different forces. But, to repeat, who can divorce slavery – its reality, its survivals, its imagined past and its mythology – from the development of modern racism?

It is difficult to disentangle the British role in black slavery from the broader canvas of British imperial history. Clearly, the slave trade and slavery left their own distinctive legacies, but they were extreme forms of a more general drive to imperial conquest and settlement. Much of that story was rapacious to a degree which is not often recognised, but the story of imperialism is not uniformly malignant, even if it is generally perceived within a context of exploitation. But it is difficult to find another episode of British imperial history which is both as rapacious and as exploitative as the history of slavery. It is that singular and, by now, well-known fact which persists as slavery's most potent legacy.

Bibliographical guide

These comments are designed to guide readers to literature that is recent, accessible and relevant. For those who want more detailed and specialised material, they could begin with the annual bibliography compiled by Joseph Miller and published in the journal *Slavery and Abolition* (Frank Cass, London). The latest version appeared in Volume 11, No. 2, September 1990, pp. 251–308. Other good general guides to recent writings on slavery (though both with an emphasis on the USA) can be found in the following: Robert W. Fogel, *Without Consent or Contract*, New York, 1989, pp. 487–523; Donald R. Wright, *African Americans in the Colonial Era*, Arlington Heights, Illinois, 1990, pp. 153–75.

1 Slavery in its context

Readers interested in classical slavery should turn to the writings of Moses Finley; *Slavery in Classical Antiquity*, Cambridge, 1968 is a good starting point. His influence can be gauged from the essays in M. L. Finley, ed., *Classical Slavery*, London, 1987. T. Wiedemann's *Greek and Roman Slavery*, London, 1981 provides a helpful guide and collection of original sources. Rodney Hilton's work on serfdom can be approached through *Bondmen Made Free*, London, 1973, but for the wider subject of medieval serfdom see Pierre Bonnassie, *From Slavery to Feudalism in South-Western Europe*, Cambridge, 1991 and Pierre Dockès, *Medieval Slavery and Liberation*, London, 1982. A wide-ranging and provocative study of slavery in its widest setting can be found in Orlando Patterson, *Slavery and Social Death*, Cambridge, Mass., 1982.

2 European expansion and the origins of black slavery

The literature on European expansion is vast – and in all the major European languages. Begin with a marvellously concise account in P. D. Curtin, *The Rise and Fall of the Plantation Complex*, Cambridge, 1990. Older, more detailed, but still important is J. H. Parry, *The Age of Reconnaissance*, London, 1963. The most recent debate on expansion can be found in Barbara Solow, ed., *Slavery and the Rise of the Atlantic System*, Cambridge, 1991. For an emphasis on the economics of expansion see Ralph Davis, *The Rise of the Atlantic Economies*, London, 1973. Stuart B. Schwartz, *Sugar Plantations in the Formation of Brazilian Society, 1550–1835*, Cambridge, 1985 traces the formative links between sugar and slavery. So too does Sidney Mintz in his masterly book, *Sweetness and Power*, London, 1985. For those interested in slavery and the slave trade in Africa, turn to Paul Lovejoy, *Transformations in Slavery: A History of Slavery in Africa*, Cambridge, 1983 and Patrick Manning, *Slavery and African Life*, Cambridge, 1990. A compact account can be found in Philip Curtin *et al.*, *African History*, London, 1978.

3 British slavery

For a general study of the Caribbean see Franklin W. Knight, *The Caribbean: The Genesis of a Fragmented Nationalism*, Oxford, 1978. Herbert Klein's *African Slavery in Latin America and the West Indies*, Oxford, 1986, is a good comparative account. James Walvin, *Black Ivory: A History of British Slavery*, London, 1992 provides a more narrative account. Those interested in the peopling of the British Americas should turn to the essays in Bernard Bailey and Philip D. Morgan, eds.,

Strangers Within the Realm: Cultural Margins of the First British Empire, Chapel Hill, 1991. R. S. Dunn, *Sugar and Slaves*, London, 1972 deals with the early years of slavery in the British Caribbean. So too does Hilary McD. Beckles, *White Servitude and Black Slavery in Barbados, 1627–1715*, Knoxville, 1989. J. P. Green's *Pursuits of Happiness*, London, 1988 provides some interesting comparative detail on the West Indian and North American colonies. For slavery in Virginia see Alan Kulikoff, *Tobacco and Slaves*, Chapel Hill, 1986. The settlement of South Carolina is dealt with best in Peter H. Wood, *Black Majority*, New York, 1974.

4 The slave trade

The standard work – and still the best – is Philip D. Curtin, *The Atlantic Slave Trade: A Census*, Madison, Wisconsin, 1969. Curtin's data has been revised by numerous historians, but his central thesis remains intact. A more descriptive account can be found in James Rawley, *The Transatlantic Slave Trade*, New York, 1981, but see also Herbert Klein, *The Middle Passage*, Princeton, 1978. David Eltis, *Economic growth and the Ending of the Transatlantic Slave Trade*, Oxford, 1987 is a monumental work: not an easy read, but well worth the effort. For the slave trade from smaller British ports see Nigel Tattersfield, *The Forgotten Trade*, London, 1991. Periodic revisions of the slave trade data appear in most of the relevant scholarly periodicals. Readers should consult Joseph Miller's annual bibliography (see above). Essays outlining the impact of the slave trade on Africa are regular features in the *Journal of African History*; see in particular those by Paul E. Lovejoy and David Richardson in Vol. 30, 1989.

5 *Slaves at work*

Slave work in the various tropical staples is described in the books by R. S. Dunn, Peter Wood and A. Kulikoff listed under Chapter 3. For rice, see also Charles Joyner, *Down by the Riverside*, Chapel Hill, 1984. For sugar, see Michael Craton, *Searching for the Invisible Man*, Cambridge, Mass., 1978. On tobacco, see T. H. Breen's *Tobacco Culture*, Princeton, 1985. The physical consequences of slave work can be judged in Richard Sheridan's book, *Doctors and Slaves*, Cambridge, 1985. The most detailed study of slaves and their work is Barry Higman's *Slave Populations of the British Caribbean*, Baltimore, 1984. J. R. Ward's *British West Indian Slavery*, Oxford, 1988 shows the improvements in British slavery during its last half-century. Mechal Sobel's study, *The World they Made Together: Black and White Values in Eighteenth Century Virginia*, Princeton, 1987 is a rich and provocative study of the inter-dependence of black and white. Slave women and their work can be found in Hilary McD. Beckles, *Natural Rebels: A Social History of Enslaved Black Women in Barbados*, London, 1989; see also Barbara Bush, *Slave Women in Caribbean Society, 1650–1838*, London, 1990. An extraordinary account of the lives of slaves, seen through the eyes of their white master, is to be found in Douglas Hall, ed., *In Miserable Slavery: Thomas Thistlewood in Jamaica, 1750–1786*, London, 1989.

6 *Slaves at rest*

This topic still awaits proper attention, though historians of North American slavery have dealt with it more adequately than those working on the Caribbean. Much good evidence is to be found in the books by Sobel, Beckles, Bush and Hall listed in Chapter 5. On North America, readers should begin with L. W. Levine, *Black Culture and Black Consciousness*, New York, 1978. John Blassingame's *The Slave Community*, New

York, 1979 affords a richly evocative account. Contemporary accounts of slaves' social activities can be found in R.D. Abrahams and J.F. Szwed, eds., *After Africa*, New Haven, 1983. The coming of Christianity among West Indian slaves is the concern of Mary Turner, *Missionaries and Slaves*, Urbana, 1985.

7 *Resistance*

Slave resistance in the British colonies is best approached through Michael Craton's *Testing the Chains*, Ithaca, 1982. The revolt in Haiti is brilliantly evoked in David Geggus, *Slavery, War and Revolution*, Oxford, 1982. More comparative is Robin Blackburn, *The Overthrow of Colonial Slavery, 1776–1848*, London, 1988. For maroon societies see Richard Price, ed., *Maroon Societies*, Baltimore, 1973. See also Gerald Mullin, *Flight and Rebellion*, New York, 1972. Slave runaways form the core of Gad Heuman's important collection of essays, *Out of the House of Bondage*, London, 1986. E.D. Genovese, *From Rebellion to Revolution*, New York, 1979 offers an impressively broad study of slave resistance. For slave resistance in the determining context of European politics and revolution, see David Brion Davis, *Slavery in the Age of Revolution*, Ithaca, 1975 and *Slavery and Human Progress*, Oxford, 1984. See also James Walvin, *England, Slaves and Freedom*, London, 1983.

8 *Ending slavery*

The debate about the ending of slavery has spawned an amazing volume of literature. Begin with the classic statement by Eric Williams, *Capitalism and Slavery*, London, 1944, various reprints. For more recent reinterpretations and disagreements with Williams, see the essays in Barbara Solow and Stanley Engerman, eds., *British Capitalism and Caribbean*

Slavery, Cambridge, 1988. The claims that the revolt in Haiti shaped the coming of black freedom are best argued in C. L. R. James, *The Black Jacobins*, New York, 1963 edn., but see also Elizabeth Fox-Genovese and E. D. Genovese, *The Fruits of Merchant Capitalism*, Oxford, 1983. A number of recent essays have sought to locate black freedom in the broader context of British social and economic change. Among the best are those by Thomas L. Haskell, David Brion Davis and John Ashworth in the *American Historical Review*, Vol. 90, April 1985 and Vol. 92, 1987. Three books in particular need to be considered: David Brion Davis, *The Problem of Slavery in the Age of Revolution*, Ithaca, 1975; Seymour Drescher, *Capitalism and Antislavery: British Mobilization in Comparative Perspective*, London, 1987 and Seymour Drescher, *Econocide: British Slavery in the Era of Abolition*, Pittsburgh, 1977.

9 *The legacy*

Some of the major results of black freedom are dealt with by the essays in Jack Hayward, ed., *Out of Slavery*, London, 1985 and David Richardson, *Abolition and its Aftermath*, London, 1985. The most important economic analysis of the ending of the slave trade is David Eltis, *Economic Growth and the Ending of the Transatlantic Slave Trade*, Oxford, 1987. Slavery and its fall in the USA is best dealt with by Robert W. Fogel, *Without Consent or Contract*, New York, 1989. For the immediate results of emancipation in the West Indies, see William A. Green, *British Slave Emancipation: The Sugar Colonies and the Great Experiment, 1830–1865*, Oxford, 1976. A broader debate on the results of abolition can be found in Christine Bolt and Seymour Drescher, eds., *Anti-Slavery, Religion and Reform*, Folkestone, 1980. The development of nineteenth-century racist thought and its links with slavery can be explored in: Peter Fryer, *Staying Power: The History of Black People in Britain*, London,

1984; Douglas A. Lorimer, *Colour, Class and the Victorians*, Leicester, 1978 and Paul B. Rich, *Race and Empire in British Politics*, Cambridge, 1986. A useful summary can be found in the essay by Seymour Drescher, 'The ending of the slave trade and the evolution of European scientific racism', *Social Science History*, Vol., 14, 1990.

Bibliography

Anstey, R. *The Atlantic Slave Trade and British Abolition, 1760–1810*. London, 1975.

—— and P. E. H. Hair, eds. *Liverpool, the African Slave Trade and Abolition*. Historical Society of Lancashire and Cheshire, 1976.

Bailyn, B. and P. D. Morgan, eds. *Strangers within the Realm*. Chapel Hill, 1991.

Beckles, H. McD. *Natural Rebels*. London, 1989.

Bernal, M. *Black Athena*. London, 1987.

Blackburn, R. *The Overthrow of Colonial Slavery*, London, 1988.

Bonnassie, P. *From Slavery to Feudalism in South-Western Europe*. Cambridge, 1991.

Characteristic Traits of the Creolian African Negroes in Jamaica (anon.). Kingston, 1797.

Checkland, S. O. and E. A. O. *The Gladstones*. Cambridge, 1974.

Craton, M. *Searching for the Invisible Man*. Cambridge, Mass., 1978.

—— *Testing the Chains*. Ithaca, 1982.

——, J. Walvin & D. Wright, eds. *Slavery, Abolition and Emancipation*. London, 1976.

Curtin, P. D. *The Atlantic Slave Trade: A Census*. Madison, Wisconsin, 1969.

—— *The Rise and Fall of the Plantation Complex*. Cambridge, 1990.

—— et al. *African History*. London, 1978.

Bibliography

Drescher, S. *Econocide: British Slavery in the Era of Abolition.* Pittsburgh, 1977.
—— *Capitalism and Antislavery.* London, 1987.
Edwards, P., ed. *Equiano's Travels.* London, 1970.
Eltis, D. *Economic Growth and the Ending of the Transatlantic Slave Trade.* Oxford, 1987.
Engerman S.L. & E.D. Genovese, eds. *Race and Slavery in the Western Hemisphere.* Princeton, 1974.
Finley, M.L., ed. *Slavery in Classical Antiquity.* Cambridge, 1968.
—— *Classical Slavery.* London, 1987.
Fogel, R. *Without Consent or Contract.* New York, 1989.
—— and S.L. Engerman *Time on the Cross.* 2 vols., New York, 1974.
Fox-Genovese, Elizabeth & E.D. Genovese *The Fruits or Merchant Capitalism.* Oxford, 1983.
Fryer, P. *Staying Power.* London, 1984.
Geggus, D. *Slavery, War and Revolution.* Oxford, 1982.
Genovese, E.D. *Roll, Jordan, Roll.* London, 1975.
—— *From Rebellion to Revolution.* New York, 1979.
Greene, J.P. *Pursuits of Happiness.* London, 1988.
Hakluyt, R. *Principal Navigations ...* (1589). 7 vols., London, 1926.
Hale, J.H. *Renaissance Europe, 1480–1520.* London, 1971.
Hayward, J., ed. *Out of Slavery.* London, 1985.
Heuman, G., ed. *Out of the House of Bondage.* London, 1986.
Higman, B. *Slave Populations of the British Caribbean.* Baltimore, 1984.
Hilton, R. *Bondmen Made Free.* London, 1973.
—— *The Decline of Serfdom,* London, 1969.
Isaac, R. *The Transformation of Virginia.* Chapel Hill, 1982.
Joyner, C. *Down by the Riverside.* Chapel Hill, 1984.
Klein, H. *The Middle Passage.* Princeton, 1978.
—— *African Slavery in Latin America and the Caribbean.* Oxford, 1986.
Kulikoff, A. *Tobacco and Slaves.* Chapel Hill, 1986.

Slaves and slavery

Lady Nugent's Journal, 1801–1805. Kingston, 1966.

Lovejoy, P.E. Transformations in slavery. Cambridge, 1983.

McKendrick, N., J. Brewer & J.H. Plumb The Birth of a Consumer Society. London, 1983.

Manning, P. Slavery and African Life. Cambridge, 1990.

Miers, S. & I. Kopytoff, eds. Slavery in Africa. Madison, Wisconsin, 1977.

Miller, J.C. Way of Death: Merchant Capitalism and the Angolan Slave Trade. London, 1988.

Mintz, S. Sweetness and Power. London, 1985.

Newton, J. Journal of a Slave Trader (1788). B. Martin and M.M. Spurrell, eds., London, 1962.

Parry, J.H. The Age of Reconaissance. London, 1963.

Patterson, O. Slavery and Social Death. Cambridge, Mass., 1982.

Price, R., ed. Maroon Societies. Baltimore, 1978.

Rawley, J. The Transatlantic Slave Trade. New York, 1981.

Rice, C. Duncan The Rise and Fall of Black Slavery. London, 1975.

Rodney, W. How Europe Underdeveloped Africa. London, 1981.

Schwartz, S. Sugar Plantations in the Formation of Brazilian Society. Cambridge, 1985.

Shammas, C. The Pre-Industrial Consumer in England and America. Oxford, 1990.

Sheridan, R. Doctors and Slaves. Cambridge, 1985.

Snowden, F., Jnr. Before Color Prejudice. Cambridge, Mass., 1983.

Sobel, M. The World they Made Together. Princeton, 1987.

Solow, B., ed. Slavery and the Rise of the Atlantic System. Cambridge, 1991.

—— and S.L. Engerman, eds. British Capitalism and Caribbean Slavery. Cambridge, 1988.

Tattersfield, N. The Forgotten Trade. London, 1991.

Tinker, H. A New System of Slavery. Oxford, 1974.

Turner, M. Missionaries and Slaves. Urbana, Ill., 1985.

Bibliography

Walvin, J. *England, Slaves and Freedom*. London, 1983.
—— *Slavery and The Slave Trade*. London, 1983.
Ward, J.R. *British West Indian Slavery*. Oxford, 1988.
Wiedemann, T. *Greek and Roman Slavery*. London, 1981.
Williams, E. *Capitalism and Slavery*. London, 1944.
Wood, P. *Black Majority*. New York, 1974.

Index

Index

Index

Index

Index